US Air Force Bases in the UK

PAUL BINGLEY

AMBERLEY

Front cover: Hangars at RAF Honington, the last USAAF air base to be returned to the RAF in 1946.

Back cover: The runway and taxiways at Woodbridge. (Richard E. Flagg)

First published 2018

Amberley Publishing
The Hill, Stroud,
Gloucestershire, GL5 4EP

www.amberley-books.com

ISBN 978 1 4456 7965 5 (print)
ISBN 978 1 4456 7966 2 (ebook)

British Library Cataloguing in Publication Data.
A catalogue record for this book is available from the British Library.

Typeset in 10pt on 13pt Celeste.
Origination by Amberley Publishing.
Printed in the UK.

Contents

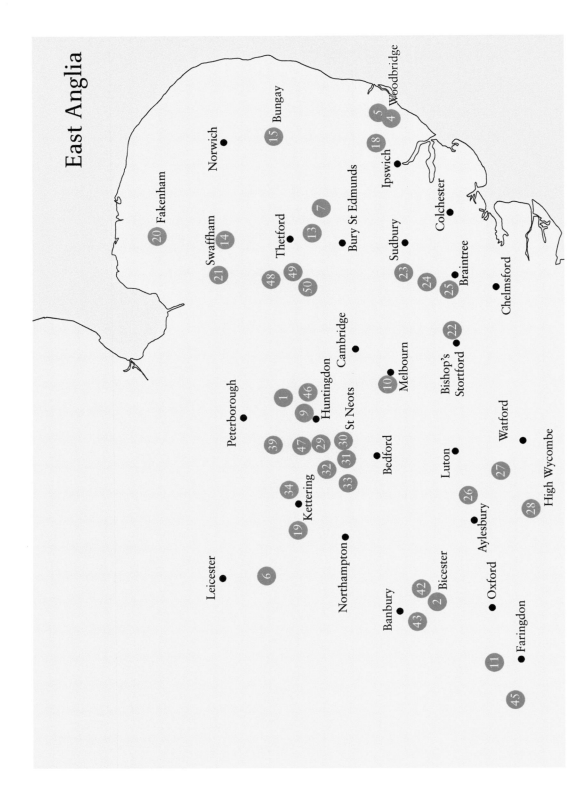

East Anglia

Woodbridge

Bungay

Norwich

Fakenham

Swaffham

Thetford

Bury St Edmunds

Ipswich

Colchester

Sudbury

Braintree

Chelmsford

Cambridge

Melbourn

Bishop's
Stortford

Watford

Huntingdon

St Neots

Peterborough

Bedford

Luton

High Wycombe

Kettering

Aylesbury

Leicester

Northampton

Bicester

Oxford

Banbury

Faringdon

4

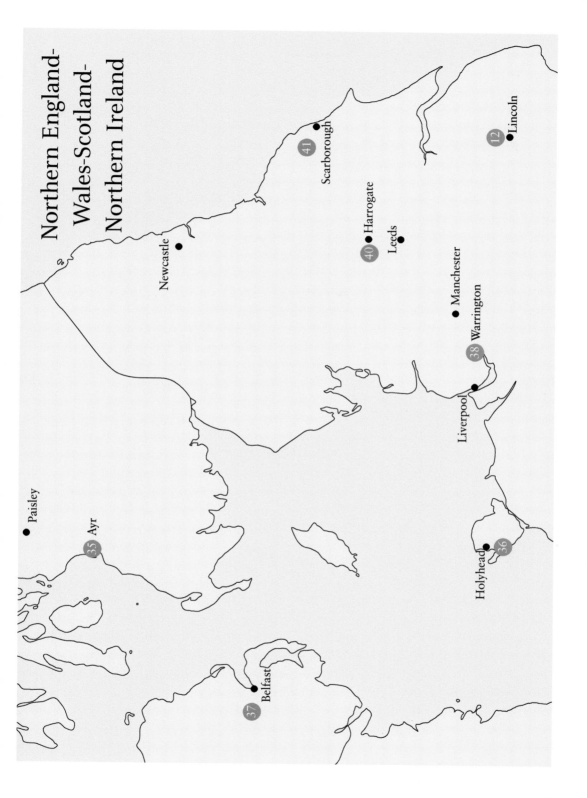

Northern England-
Wales-Scotland-
Northern Ireland

Lincoln

12

Scarborough

41

Harrogate

40

Leeds

Newcastle

Manchester

Warrington

38

Liverpool

Paisley

Ayr

35

Holyhead

36

Belfast

37

South-Southeast England

Margate

Ashford

Maidstone

London

Reading

Newbury

Southampton

Bournemouth

6

Map Legend

1. Upwood
2. Upper Heyford
3. Greenham Common
4. Woodbridge
5. Bentwaters
6. Bruntingthorpe
7. Shepherds Grove
8. Manston
9. Wyton
10. Bassingbourn
11. Brize Norton
12. Scampton
13. Honington
14. North Pickenham
15. Hardwick
16. Lashenden
17. Christchurch
18. Debach
19. Harrington
20. Sculthorpe
21. Marham
22. Stansted Mountfitchet
23. Ridgewell
24. Wethersfield
25. Andrews Field
26. Cheddington
27. Bovingdon
28. 'Pinetree'
29. Kimbolton
30. Little Staughton
31. Thurleigh
32. Chelveston
33. Podington
34. Grafton Underwood
35. Prestwick
36. Valley
37. Nutts Corner
38. Burtonwood
39. Polebrook
40. Menwith Hill
41. Fylingdales
42. Croughton
43. Barford St. John
44. Welford
45. Fairford
46. Alconbury
47. Molesworth
48. Feltwell
49. Lakenheath
50. Mildenhall

Preface

On 19 May 1943, British Prime Minister Winston Churchill rose to his feet to deliver his second address to a joint session of Congress in Washington. Acknowledging the Allies' victory in the North African campaign six days earlier, he made a prescient remark:

> We have certainly a most encouraging example here of what can be achieved by British and Americans working together heart and hand. In fact, one might almost feel that if they could keep it up, there is hardly anything they could not do, either in the field of war or in the not less tangled problems of peace.

Churchill's speech came on the day that the Allies rubber-stamped the terms of the Combined Bomber Offensive. A growing number of airfields across the British Isles were reverberating to the sound of American aircraft by day, and British by night. Almost exactly two years later, however, many of those airfields suddenly fell silent. Bombers were replaced by tractors, and farmland reclaimed their runways.

But for a brief lull in 1946, a handful of British airfields have hosted aircraft of the United States Air Force ever since. They remain concrete evidence of the 'special relationship' lauded by Churchill after the war. Yet, many more have melted into the landscape – ghostly outlines of a seismic shift in British history.

This book doesn't seek to cover every UK airfield used by the Americans (there are too many to adequately describe), neither does it focus on their support facilities – some 300 of which helped the Americans mount their wartime campaign. Rather, it merely chronicles the circumstances under which many of those airfields first appeared, and what has become of some of them since. It also examines the continued American presence on British soil today.

From the Second World War, through the Berlin Airlift, to the 'War on Terror', the UK has continued to serve as a 'vast aircraft carrier anchored off the north-west coast of Europe'. This book examines how the 'special relationship' has helped shape the land we see today.

Foreword

During the Second World War, much of the eastern side of England became home to vast numbers of airfields, filled with bombers, fighters and the hundreds of thousands of men – and women – needed to keep these fleets and their crews in the air. Each airfield was, in many ways, its own small town, springing up almost as if by magic; where once there had been a small farm growing wheat, barley and sugar beet, now suddenly there were Americans and Canadians and airmen from all around the world, as well as from British shores, populating a mass of buildings, huts and hangars and paving a mass of roadways that once had been country paths and tracks. It was an extraordinary transformation that is barely comprehensible today.

Both Britain and the United States entered the war with air power at the forefront of their strategy for victory. This was part of the 'steel not flesh' policy in which they were determined to use their global reach, industrial capacity and huge advances in technology to create arms and machinery that would rain destruction on their enemies at minimal cost to the lives of their own young men. Of course, the casualties were still enormously high but broadly the strategy worked as Allied losses were far less than any of the other major combatants and that was in no way because of the lack of effort or commitment. Of course, losses to aircrew were particularly horrific, but for all the moral arguments about mass bombing, there was no question that air power, in all its many forms, made a massive contribution to the eventual Allied victory that came in 1945.

The importance of air power swiftly extended into the peace that followed – a peace that soon looked horribly fragile and quickly developed into the Cold War. During the war, huge strides had been made in aeronautical technology, not least with the development of jet power. First Britain then America began to develop new and powerful aircraft that were at the cutting edge of world technological developments. Over a war-torn and tired Britain, incredible ultra-modern jet aircraft of fantastical shapes and designs were suddenly screaming across the skies at the kind of shattering speeds that just a few years earlier had been unthinkable.

At the war's end, Britain had granted the newly independent US Air Force permission to temporarily remain on some of the bases from which they had operated during the war, a deal that was repeatedly extended, so that while most of the old Second World War airfields were handed back and turned back to farmland, a number remained and were further expanded. These important bases have since then played witness to the evolution and development of the USAF and its combat and defence role within Europe. Heavy bombers, fast jets, spy planes and some of the most powerful and technologically advanced aircraft ever built have flown from these bases, as Paul Bingley charts in this timely and important book.

Now, however, the era of the American air power in the UK is drawing to a close. From the millions of American air servicemen and women that once served here there remains just a handful, now operating from a small number of remaining bases. Some of those are due to close within the next few years.

The aviation heritage in this country is a rich one, and, since 1942, has been shared with the air forces of the United States. It is important, though, to appreciate and understand that it was a relationship that did not stop with the end of the Second World War but has continued ever since, as this fascinating and beautifully illustrated book reminds us so vividly.

James Holland

CHAPTER ONE

Firm Footings

The first few steps taken by the nascent United States Air Force (USAF) in Great Britain began on 26 June 1917, when Raynal C. Bolling, a major of the Aviation Section of the US Signal Corps, set foot on Liverpool's quay.

Just over two months earlier, the United States had entered the First World War with little experience in aircraft manufacturing or combat use. Bolling had then been tasked with leading an aeronautical group to study the latest in British and French aircraft design. The 'Bolling Commission' visited a number of British aerodromes to inspect the Royal Flying Corps' fighters before moving on to France for an evaluation of French aircraft. Bolling himself, however, was fated never to return home. After being ambushed by German soldiers, he became the first high-ranking American officer to be killed in the conflict.

Major Raynal C. Bolling, a successful New York City lawyer, was one of the first American military airmen to set foot in the United Kingdom during the First World War. (Author's Collection)

Bolling's work preceded the earliest collaboration between the British and American air forces. Just two weeks before his death, cadets of the American 165th Aero Squadron had arrived at Fowlmere aerodrome in Cambridgeshire to begin training under the instruction of the newly named Royal Air Force (RAF). The 165th had been established as a 'day bombardment squadron' and quickly found itself deployed to the Western Front as part of the Air Service of the American Expeditionary Forces. It wasn't the first, however. Other American units had already been attached to British squadrons before transferring alongside them to France. Nevertheless, by 1919, most had been disbanded.

Following the Armistice in November 1918, the need for British aerodromes also diminished. Fowlmere saw its four aeroplane sheds and camp buildings demolished, and by 1923 little of the base remained. Few could have predicted the significant role this airfield would play in another looming conflict.

After analysing the effects of aerial bombing during the First World War, many world leaders, concerned with its destructive capability, moved to ban the bomber. Nevertheless, conscious of Germany's clandestine rearmament, the policy was soon shelved. Between 1934 and 1939, the British Government oversaw an airfield expansion programme that evolved through a series of alphabetical 'schemes'. It was a period that sparked the large-scale reconstruction of disused stations, while 100 new airfields were also established. When Britain declared war on Germany on 3 September 1939, a further 110 civil aerodromes were requisitioned, bringing the total number of airfields available for military use to 270.

The new 'expansion scheme' aerodromes were characterised by their neo-Georgian facades and plush officers' messes. Building plans had to be approved by the Royal Fine Arts Commission, while the location for new airfields involved consultation with the Society for the Preservation of Rural England. One airfield that predated the period was RAF Mildenhall in Suffolk.

Land had been purchased by the British Government in 1929. By 1931, the first buildings were constructed. Initially known as Beck Row, its name was changed to Mildenhall two years later. On 19 October 1934, King George V officially dedicated the airfield, returning the following year to review 350 aircraft on the occasion of his Silver Jubilee. Four years later, on the same day that Britain declared war on Germany, three Wellington bombers climbed away from its runways in search of German warships at Wilhelmshaven. They formed part of RAF Bomber Command's first operational sortie of the Second World War. From these beginnings, Mildenhall's is an exceptional story that continues to the present day.

By the time of RAF Bomber Command's first foray into Nazi-occupied Europe, the fledgling USAF – then known as the US Army Air Corps – could call upon just 1,200 combat aircraft and 22,700 personnel. It ranked a mere twentieth in size in the world. Its strength, however, became largely irrelevant when the US President, Franklin D. Roosevelt, publicly declared American neutrality two days later. Nevertheless, mindful of the threat that the Nazi regime posed to the United States, Roosevelt asked Congress to substantially raise the national defence budget. He also urged the American aircraft industry to increase its production from 2,000 aircraft a year to more than 4,000 per month. When he was elected for a third term on 5 November 1940, Roosevelt immediately offered the British twenty newly designed Boeing bombers.

Known by the Americans as the 'Flying Fortress', the B-17 was less than enthusiastically received by the RAF. Deputy Chief of the Air Staff, Arthur Harris, had written a scathing report in which he'd likened its nose dome to something 'more appropriately located in an amusement park than in a war plane'. Despite his misgivings, however, the British Government accepted the offer. Five months later, the first B-17C landed on British soil.

No. 90 Squadron (RAF) had been reformed to operate the bomber – known as 'Fortress I' by the British. To assist the squadron with its familiarisation, a cadre of US Army Air Corps (USAAC) officers had secretly accompanied the bombers to England. One of those was Lieutenant Foley Bradley, who purportedly became the first USAAC officer to be killed on active duty when his B-17 disintegrated in bad weather over Catterick, Yorkshire.

Major General James E. Chaney, another American airman and 'special army observer', had already begun inspecting sites for possible American installations a month earlier. One of the airfields under consideration was at Polebrook in Northamptonshire. On 28 June 1941, after negotiating unfinished hardstands and taxiways on a site that had previously been a potato patch, No. 90 Squadron's B-17Cs arrived at the airfield. It was from here that they would carry out the first of thousands of Flying Fortress raids on Europe. Polebrook wouldn't just have the distinction of introducing the B-17 into combat – it would also become one of the first British bases to help steer the Americans towards Nazi Germany.

By the time of Polebrook's introduction, the USAAC had been re-designated the United States Army Air Forces (USAAF). Almost immediately a group of its officers set off to inspect other airfields across the United Kingdom. They quickly found that Burtonwood in Lancashire was ideally situated, lying just 15 miles from the Port of Liverpool – the chief entry point for imported fuel, food and raw materials into the UK. Burtonwood would prove to be an outstanding logistical hub. However, on 7 December 1941, American attention was abruptly drawn away from Great Britain, and the war in Europe.

'A date which will live in infamy' was how Franklin Roosevelt announced the surprise Japanese attack on Pearl Harbor. Almost immediately an Anglo-American conference was convened in Washington to assess the threat posed by both Japan and Germany. Despite

Having observed the Battle of Britain and the London Blitz, Major General James E. Chaney was formally assigned to the UK in May 1941 as a Special Army Observer. Chaney was responsible for surveying potential US installations, including RAF Polebrook. (Author's Collection)

A B-17C (Fortress I) of RAF No. 90 Squadron takes off from a partly constructed RAF Polebrook on 24 July 1941 to attack the German battleship *Gneisenau*. No. 90 Squadron's B-17s (and Polebrook) were inspected by the American Special Army Observer James E. Chaney. (© Crown Copyright IWM)

The 'Stars and Stripes' are raised at RAF Burtonwood on 22 October 1943. Burtonwood was destined to become the largest USAAF airfield in Europe during the Second World War. (Author's Collection)

the unfolding situation in the Pacific, Hitler's subsequent declaration of war on the US prodded Roosevelt into a 'Germany first' strategy. The Allies' Combined Chiefs of Staff soon began directing the war effort towards Europe. Their first undertaking was to approve the despatch of an American bomber force to join the RAF's Bomber Command.

Over the course of several weeks in early 1942, a number of USAAF bomb groups were established to prepare for movement to England. Shortly afterwards, the first mass movement of American ground troops began arriving in Northern Ireland. They were the vanguard for over two million American personnel eventually posted to the UK during the Second World War.

American engineers lay cement to improve Molesworth's runways and taxiways in early July 1943. Molesworth had already benefitted from Ira Eaker's inspection in 1942, but it continued to be upgraded. (Author's Collection)

A few weeks later, the USAAF's Eighth Air Force was activated at Savannah, Georgia. It initially comprised three units – VIII Bomber Command, VIII Fighter Command and VIII Ground Air Services Command. Appointed Commanding General of VIII Bomber Command, Brigadier General Ira C. Eaker was immediately ordered to proceed to England. Shortly after his arrival, he and his staff travelled to Molesworth in Huntingdonshire.

Molesworth had previously been a Royal Flying Corps landing ground during the First World War. Following its reconstruction in the months before Eaker's visit, the airfield had then hosted the Royal Australian Air Force and RAF. Eaker's inspection would significantly alter the airfield's layout. Its runways were subsequently lengthened and the number of hardstands increased to accommodate the larger American heavy bomb groups. Molesworth would prove to be the template for many other heavy bomber bases that followed.

The USAAF initially estimated that sixteen heavy bomb groups, three fighter groups and eight photo-reconnaissance squadrons would be sent to the UK during 1942. It also projected that each group would occupy a single airfield, with three groups forming a combat wing and five combat wings comprising a single bombardment wing. VIII Bomber Command was expected to control a total of five bombardment wings. On 1 March 1942, the 92nd Bombardment Group became the first heavy bomber unit to be formally activated.

Scores of airfields throughout the UK were soon being tentatively allocated to the Eighth Air Force. Several were located in Northern Ireland – one of which was at Nutts Corner near Belfast. This former civilian airfield had been turned over to RAF Coastal Command in 1941. It had then been expanded and upgraded for RAF Liberator operations against German U-boats. Nutts Corner, together with Prestwick in Scotland and Valley in Wales, was primed to become one of the first landfall sites for American bombers arriving after their North Atlantic crossings.

By the end of March 1942, a further eight British airfields were assigned to host the first bomb groups set to arrive from the United States. After Eaker's extensive survey of East Anglian sites, Grafton Underwood, Podington and Chelveston in Northamptonshire; Thurleigh (Bedfordshire); Little Staughton (Cambridgeshire); and Kimbolton (Huntingdonshire) were

A Douglas C-54 Skymaster lifts off from RAF Prestwick loaded with wounded GIs bound for the US. Prestwick had the distinction of welcoming the first B-17E during 'Operation BOLERO', and, in 1960, US Army Specialist 4 Elvis Presley. (Author's Collection)

Welsh civilians wave farewell to the departing B-24 *Glory Bee* as she taxis at RAF Valley, bound for the United States. Valley was a major transit hub for bombers flown across the Atlantic Ocean. (Author's Collection)

all selected to join Polebrook and Molesworth in becoming the first American bases. Many of them, however, were still undergoing some form of construction.

On 12 April 1942, the Commanding General of the USAAF, Henry H. Arnold, submitted a report to the US Army's Chief of Staff, General George Marshall, which was to be the basis for 'Operation BOLERO' – the codename for the American military build-up in the United Kingdom. Forty-eight hours later, 'BOLERO' was formally accepted by the British Government.

Engineers of the first Eighth Air Force heavy bomb group to be activated – the 92nd – work on a lone B-17 in one of Podington's two T2 hangars. Both hangars have since been removed. (Author's Collection)

Still under construction in July 1943, Chelveston eventually welcomed the 305th Bomb Group. Nicknamed the 'Can Do' group, the 305th pioneered many of the Eighth Air Force's early bombing techniques. (Author's Collection)

Thurleigh's perimeter track starting to show signs of wear and tear after its early use by B-17s of the 306th Bomb Group. Thurleigh would remain in combat use longer than any other airfield. (Author's Collection)

Despite the appearance of airfields in many rural areas, the British soon grew accustomed to the 'Yanks' and their strange-looking machines. Here, a group of children crowd around a B-17 at RAF Kimbolton. (Author's Collection)

Days later, Ira Eaker relocated his headquarters to Wycombe Abbey – a requisitioned girls' school in Buckinghamshire. Codenamed 'Pinetree' and given the USAAF station number 101, it was sited just 5 miles from RAF Bomber Command's headquarters at High Wycombe. Wycombe Abbey's governors were given just three weeks' notice to remove their 250 pupils before its grounds were fortified with an underground bunker stretching across three floors. Comprising concrete protection and an air conditioning and filtration system designed to maintain a high air pressure to protect against gas attack, it was from 'Pinetree' that all Eighth Air Force missions would be directed for the rest of the war.

Codenamed 'Pinetree', Wycombe Abbey girls' school was requisitioned by VIII Bomber Command and used to plan the Eighth Air Force's early missions, including the famous Schweinfurt-Regensburg raid on 17 August 1943. (J. RossGreene)

On 27 April 1942, the first large-scale movement of American airmen set sail from Boston. Among the 1,800 men aboard was an advanced echelon of the Eighth Air Force Headquarters, commanded by Major General Carl A. Spaatz, a veteran combat airman who'd led an Aero Squadron during the First World War. Spaatz and his men reached England twenty-four hours before the 15th Bomb Squadron, which arrived at Grafton Underwood after a lengthy journey from Australia. The 15th duly became the first American bomber unit to arrive in the UK – albeit without any aircraft.

In early June 1942, the British Air Ministry issued a list of twenty-eight airfields to be transferred to VIII Bomber Command. In addition to the eight already allocated, the inventory included a further twenty in the eastern counties, including RAF Bovingdon in Hertfordshire. Bovingdon had been assigned to become a major American bomber training base with the primary mission of supporting the nearby Eighth Air Force Headquarters. RAF Cheddington in Buckinghamshire, a former First World War aerodrome, was also tasked with receiving and training American bomber crews.

Later that same month, elements of the 97th Bomb Group began arriving at the reconstructed Polebrook. Now enlarged with extended runways and hardstands, the first airfield to host the first combat B-17s of the war duly welcomed the first American heavy bomb group to England. The 97th's B-17Es touched down at Polebrook two weeks later.

The USAAF was anticipating a strength of 3,266 aircraft by 1 April 1943 – a figure reflected in the publication of a revised list of airfields to be allocated to the Eighth Air Force. The Air Ministry confirmed that eighty-seven would need to be readied. However,

Bovingdon in Hertfordshire became a heavy bomber training base, providing theatre indoctrination for new groups arriving in England. Here, a waist gunner tests new bulletproof clothing in November 1942. (Author's Collection)

the ever-changing battleground forced further amendments when several Eighth Air Force groups were transferred to the North African Theatre. Despite this, a significant number of airfields were still to be constructed, and among them was Great Saling in Essex.

The Air Ministry's Directorate General of Works was responsible for selecting new sites before issuing any orders for airfield construction. Like many locations proposed for bomber airfields, the preparation for Great Saling involved a furtive inspection followed by the swift requisitioning of its land and buildings. Initial groundworks then required the felling of trees and the strengthening of roads to carry an army of construction vehicles.

Great Saling was planned to be built to the RAF's 'Class A' standard – a design criteria that had been modified over two years to keep pace with the latest in aircraft design and performance. By the summer of 1942, 'Class A' was intended for any aircraft type then in service or under development. Three intersecting runways, a 3-mile perimeter track and over fifty hardstands were due to be built on the airfield. However, unlike many airfields, where British civil contractors were invited to tender for the work, Great Saling would be constructed (and renamed) under entirely different circumstances.

In July 1942, the US Army's 819th Engineer Battalion arrived at the site to begin construction. Over the next few months, its American engineers slept in tents while working through the night aided only by screened lights. Within five months the runways had been laid, and six months later the airfield was ready for use. Great Saling became the first of fourteen British airfields to be built by American engineers during the Second World War. It was also renamed RAF Andrews Field in honour of the Commanding General of the US Army in the European Theatre, Lieutenant General Frank M. Andrews, who was killed in

19

Andrews Field, the first British airfield constructed by the Americans, was also the only one to be named after an American individual. Pictured here in late 1942, the US Army lays one of its runways. (Author's Collection)

a B-24 crash in Iceland on 3 May 1943. Fittingly, Andrews Field – the first American-built airfield in the UK – became the only one to be named after an American individual.

By August 1942 a substantial number of airfields were officially handed over to the USAAF, although many were not yet fully built, nor utilised, until later in the war. Wethersfield was scheduled for completion in December 1942, but the airfield construction programme taking place across the country had entered a crisis. Severe labour shortages and a lack of resources led to Wethersfield's men and materials being diverted elsewhere midway through its construction. With three runways laid, the remainder of the airfield wasn't finished until the following winter.

Although the Germans were not fully aware of the challenges being faced by the British and Americans, they gave a hint of their knowledge in mid-August 1942. Taunting messages were dropped on both Polebrook and Grafton Underwood, demanding to know where the American bombers were. On 17 August 1942, the 97th Bomb Group duly replied. It despatched the first American B-17s from British soil for an attack on Rouen's marshalling yard. Ira Eaker took part in that first Eighth Air Force mission, flying from Polebrook in a B-17E aptly named *Yankee Doodle*.

By the end of August 1942, three heavy bomb groups, two fighter groups, two troop carrier groups and a total of 386 aircraft had arrived in the United Kingdom. The USAAF also had a plethora of new airfields to choose from. Bovingdon had been officially transferred to the Americans, along with Greenham Common and Abbots Ripton – the latter more commonly known as Alconbury.

B-17E 41-9023 *Yankee Doodle* of the 414th Bomb Squadron, 97th Bomb Group, undergoes maintenance after being one of the lead bombers on the Eighth Air Force's first heavy bomber mission on 17 August 1942. (Author's Collection)

Alconbury was then in use with RAF Bomber Command. Shortly afterwards, the first American B-24 Liberator unit to arrive in England (the 93rd Bomb Group) landed at the airfield. To facilitate its arrival, Alconbury's three runways had been extended and twenty-six new hardstands built. Two months later, King George VI visited the airfield to inspect his first Eighth Air Force base. Today, much like Mildenhall, Alconbury's is an ongoing story.

By September 1942, an average of one airfield was being handed over to the British Government every three days. Approximately sixty-three airfields had received major upgrades to runways and hardstands carried out by some 60,000 men. Nevertheless, progress remained slow, and a wet autumn combined with labour shortages continued to hinder construction. Despite the delays, however, the Americans were struggling to keep pace.

VIII Bomber Command was expecting a total of seventy-five groups, only nine of which had arrived by the beginning of November 1942. This figure was then reduced to seven when the Twelfth Air Force was activated as part of 'Operation TORCH' – the planned Anglo-American invasion of French North Africa. Around 27,000 men and 1,200 aircraft were syphoned from the Eighth Air Force and sent to North Africa, including those of the 310th Bombardment Group, which briefly passed through Hardwick in Norfolk on its way to Algeria. At the same time, the Ninth Air Force was established in the Middle East to support the growing desert campaign, although it would eventually find itself relocated to England.

By now, around 15,000 men were being conscripted into the British armed forces each month, which further eroded the labour force required to build new airfields. In December 1942, the British Government suspended all new works not associated with 'BOLERO'. Many sites that had already been requisitioned, were indefinitely mothballed. Others that had been constructed, were still waiting for their new tenants to complete their training in the United States. The British subsequently requested that ten airfields in East Anglia be released back to the RAF. Ridgewell in Essex was one, and it was thus handed to a homeless RAF squadron seeking an operational base for its new bombers.

No. 90 Squadron – the first to fly the Flying Fortress in Europe – had been reformed to carry out operations using Britain's first four-engine bomber, the Short Stirling. Arriving at RAF Ridgewell on 29 December 1942, the first Stirling to christen its newly concreted runways bounced and careered into a ditch. It was an inauspicious start.

Ridgewell's construction had taken over one million man hours. A million cubic yards of concrete, 24 miles of drains, 6 miles of water mains and more than 500 buildings had been built. Like many 'Class A' airfields, it was designed to accommodate almost 3,000 men, but when the ground crews of No. 90 Squadron arrived, they found themselves knee-deep in mud at an airfield still under construction. Despite these difficulties, however, No. 90 Squadron re-joined the war on 8 January 1943 – its first mission heralding the start of Ridgewell's legacy as Essex's only long-term heavy bomber base.

Three weeks later, Major General Ira Eaker – then commander of the Eighth Air Force – put his case for 'round-the-clock' bombing to Winston Churchill. It led to the development of the Combined Bomber Offensive, which eventually saw the Americans bomb by day and the RAF by night. A week later, the First and Second Bombardment Wings of the Eighth Air Force struck Germany for the first time. By the end of the month, over a two-day period more than 2,000 Anglo-American sorties were flown against enemy targets. It signalled the start of strategic bombing in Europe.

Photographed by the RAF's No. 1 Photographic Reconnaissance Unit in April 1942, RAF Ridgewell begins to take shape. It would go on to become Essex's only long-term heavy bomber base. (Author's Collection)

By this time, the Air Ministry had fifty-four bomber airfields under construction, in addition to those being built by American engineering battalions. Fourteen bomb groups had also reached England. More remarkably, the USAAF had grown from 354,000 men on the day of the Pearl Harbor attack to over two million in the space of just eighteen months. Over 100,000 had now arrived in the UK, representing an increase of 70 per cent in just six months. The rising tide of American bombers now circling the patchwork of East Anglian fields forced VIII Bomber Command to issue a requirement for its groups to be identified by individual markings. Taking the idea from the brand marks of American cattle ranches, each group's aircraft were soon identified by a geometric shape surrounding an individual letter. Triangles, circles and squares now adorned the Eighth Air Force's heavy bombers in a bid to help the crews recognise each other in the increasingly crowded British skies.

To cope with the growing number of damaged bombers also returning from Europe, the first of three specialised airfields was built in July 1943. Woodbridge was planned as an 'emergency landing ground', capable of accepting distressed aircraft. Owing to its coastal location it was virtually fog-free. It also enjoyed an uninterrupted east-west approach path after a million trees were felled in Rendlesham Forest. Equipped with a single 9,000-foot heavy-duty runway, with a width five times the size of a standard one, Woodbridge accepted its first 'customer' later that month. By the end of the war, it was the busiest of the emergency landing grounds, with approximately 4,120 aircraft making emergency landings – including an errant Luftwaffe Junkers JU-88, whose pilot mistook Britain for Germany.

By August 1943, the projected figure of forty-six bomb groups had been increased to fifty-six. It led to concern over the number of airfields then available. The possibility of a fourth division in the Essex/Suffolk area was mooted, but shortly afterwards another fifteen

A still image taken by the RAF's Film Production Unit showing RAF Woodbridge's vast emergency runway surrounded by Rendlesham Forest. Over 4,000 emergency landings were made at Woodbridge during the Second World War. (© Crown Copyright IWM)

The origins of the UK's fourth busiest airport began in August 1942. Here, engineers of the 817th Engineering Battalion begin surveying the site for an airfield that would later become known as RAF Stansted Mountfitchet. (Author's Collection)

groups were transferred to the Mediterranean. One Essex airfield that had been completed was Stansted Mountfitchet. Built by several American engineering battalions in 1943, it was officially opened on 7 August of that year. In addition to serving as an operational bomber base, Stansted – as it would more commonly be known – was primarily used as a maintenance and supply depot.

On 13 September 1943, VIII Bomber Command's combat wings were divided into three divisions. The First was predominantly sited on the western edge of East Anglia, the Second to the north of the region and the Third in the south. The three divisions could now call upon scores of heavy bomb groups from a swathe of airfields stretching across seven counties. The heavy bomber airfields were also complemented by four medium bomber bases in Essex, and nine fighter grounds, extending from Northamptonshire into Suffolk.

By now, VIII Ground Air Services Command had formed the basis for a new USAAF organisation assigned to the United Kingdom – the Ninth Air Force – which had recently been transferred from North Africa. Its primary purpose was to support Allied forces on the ground in the lead up to a planned Continental invasion. By mid-October 1943, more than 100 units and around thirty airfields in England were reassigned from the Eighth Air Force to the Ninth.

Although most Ninth Air Force light and medium bomb groups would subsequently be based in the south-east of England, its fighter and troop carrier wings were largely concentrated at airfields west of London (considered the most appropriate staging area for ground troops tasked with taking part in a cross-Channel invasion). Thus, new airfields like Fairford, Greenham Common and Welford were allocated to the Ninth in quick succession.

British airfields across the land were now heaving under every type of American military aircraft, including transporters, photo reconnaissance, fighters and bombers. When Sir Archibald Sinclair, Secretary of State for Air, addressed the Houses of Parliament on 29 February 1944, he acknowledged the sacrifices being made to accommodate them:

> Four and a half years ago we started the most gigantic civil engineering and building programme ever undertaken in the country ... [dispossessing] the people of their land, their homes and their crops, often with little notice and with no reprieve. It has not been a pleasant thing for the people of this country to have had their land turned into an airbase. I'm glad to say that we have almost reached the end of our territorial demands. Since the war began, working mainly through building and civil engineering contractors, it has erected one million buildings and laid down concrete tracks equivalent to a 30-foot road running from here to Peking.

Nevertheless, construction hadn't ceased altogether. One airfield that was neither assigned to the Eighth Air Force, nor the Ninth, but would ultimately play a key role in the future of the USAAF, was Marham in Norfolk.

Having opened in April 1937, Marham had then hosted a variety of RAF bomber squadrons before being closed in March 1944. Shortly afterwards, work began on redeveloping it to 'very heavy bomber' standards. Its runways were extended by 50 per cent and widened by 50 feet. Two months later, similar work was undertaken at both Lakenheath and Sculthorpe. All three were being primed to accept the first Boeing B-29 Superfortress bombers expected to be sent to the UK.

Another unique airfield allocated to the Eighth at the time of Marham's reconstruction was Harrington in Northamptonshire. Selected for its proximity to Holme – a packing and storage facility key to the Allies' resistance support – Harrington became the most westerly of the Eighth Air Force's combat bases. Originally built by two American engineering battalions for the RAF, Harrington was subsequently handed back to the Eighth Air Force in March 1944. The 801st Bombardment Group (Provisional), with its black-painted B-24 Liberators, was soon dropping supplies to resistance fighters across Nazi-occupied Europe. By the war's end, the 801st would officially become known as the 492nd Bomb Group, but informally recognised as the 'Carpetbaggers'.

One of the last heavy bomber bases to be occupied by the Eighth Air Force in England – Debach – was just a stone's throw from the emergency landing ground at Woodbridge. This new Suffolk airfield had been built by an American engineering battalion before opening in April 1944. Unlike most American-built airfields, however, Debach's runways soon began to crumble under the weight of the 493rd Bomb Group's Liberators. The group was forced to relocate to Little Walden at the end of 1944, and its aircraft would not return to Debach until two months before VE Day.

Throughout April 1944, a number of temporary airfields were opened for elements of the Ninth Air Force. Intended as prototype 'advanced landing grounds' (ALGs), they were mainly sited along the English Channel coast to provide tactical air support for the Allied invasion forces.

A black-painted B-24 Liberator of the 492nd Bomb Group, nicknamed *Miss Fitts*, takes off from RAF Harrington for another supply drop over Nazi-occupied Europe. (© Crown Copyright IWM)

Eleanor, a P-51 of the 353rd Fighter Group's 352nd Fighter Squadron, pictured alongside other P-51s and the 493rd Bomb Group's B-17s at RAF Debach in November 1944. Not long after this photograph was taken, Debach was closed for repair. (Author's Collection)

Engineers of the 833rd Engineering Battalion begin laying a mesh track at RAF Christchurch – a prototype Advanced Landing Ground (ALG). Its runways would be in wartime use for just two months. (Author's Collection)

One of them – Christchurch in Dorset – had been a private airfield and aircraft factory before the war. Allocated to the USAAF in 1943, it was deemed too small to accommodate the required runway length. In October 1943, a nearby river was diverted to reclaim land, upon which RAF engineers built a 4,800-foot strip. The RAF then made way for an American engineering battalion, which subsequently overlaid a mesh track. On 4 April 1944, the 405th Fighter Group's P-47s landed at Christchurch – a reconstructed airfield they would use for only two months.

Among the assortment of other ALGs also opened in the south-east corner of England, Ashford, Headcorn, High Halden, Lashenden, Staplehurst and Woodchurch (all in Kent) received their first Ninth Air Force units during April 1944. Much like Christchurch, their runways were built and extended using a variety of methods: square mesh track, prefabricated bituminous surfacing, pierced steel planking and Sommerfeld tracking, etc. These innovatively built airfields were intended as guides for the many that would be built (and rebuilt) in France following the Continental invasion. However, many of the British ALGs were used by the USAAF for only a matter of weeks.

With the transfer of RAF North Pickenham to the USAAF, the occupancy of all planned Eighth Air Force bases in the UK was completed. Its handover came just twelve days before D-Day. This late period 'Class A' airfield was unusual in that most of its fifty looped hardstands and single pan were confined to just one side of the airfield. It was also one of the more ill-fated, when its first incumbents, the 492nd Bomb Group, lost fifty-one B-24s during a three-month period.

Buildings at RAF Ashford in Kent, home of the 406th Fighter Group. Two weeks after its first mission on 9 May 1944, Ashford was struck by the Luftwaffe. Fourteen people lost their lives. The 406th moved to a new ALG at Tour-en-Bessin in France in August 1944. (© Crown Copyright IWM)

Pictured at High Halden in June 1944, *Chunky*, a P-47 Thunderbolt of the 365th Fighter Squadron, 358th Fighter Group, has its engine 'pulled through' by a ground crew. (Author's Collection)

Lieutenant Julian Morford of the 405th Fighter Group, pictured with his P-47 at Christchurch's Advance Landing Ground (ALG) just after D-Day. Two months later, having transferred to a newly built ALG at Picauville in France, Lt Morford was killed in action. (© Crown Copyright IWM)

B-24 44-40317 *Ruthless Ruthie* after her right landing gear collapsed during take-off from North Pickenham on 16 April 1945. North Pickenham was the last of the British airfields handed over to the Eighth Air Force during the Second World War. (Author's Collection)

After the formation of the Ninth Air Force, the Eighth had forty-two airfields to its name. It also had forty heavy bomb groups and a total of 3,000 B-17s and B-24s, mostly operating from Norfolk and Suffolk. Across 3,200 square miles of East Anglia, it was estimated that there was one airfield for every 8 miles.

On 7 June 1944, the first Allied airstrip was constructed in Normandy. Within four days, thirty-one squadrons had been transferred from the UK to France. RAF Lashenden (one of the prototype ALGs in Kent) saw the 354th Fighter Group take off from its runways on 13 June, bringing its use as an operational airfield to a swift end. It was a similar story at dozens of other bases, many of which were immediately handed back to the RAF when the Ninth Air Force began moving across the English Channel.

Following the surrender of the German High Command a year later, scores of USAAF bases were promptly returned to the RAF. Within a year, the majority of those still in use were finally relinquished from American control altogether. A huge social change, which had begun in the towns and villages of the UK three years before, gradually came to a close.

On 31 August 1945, the journal *The Aeroplane* published an article examining the spread of airfields across the UK, citing it as 'the largest constructional programme in British history'. It estimated that around £600 million had been spent by the Air Ministry on airfield construction during the first five years of the war. Around 450 new airfields had been established, covering approximately 360,000 acres of land, either pre-owned or requisitioned by the government. It represented an area the size of the county of Bedfordshire.

Nevertheless, the majority weren't built to last. Many new airfields – especially those built for the Americans – were only designed to be temporary. Yet the USAAF's absence from British soil following the end of the war would also be short term. Its footings were firm. They would soon be cemented.

CHAPTER TWO

A Concrete Presence

With the Second World War finally over, the RAF began surveying the huge number of airfields left at its disposal. Detailed site plans were drawn up depicting their layouts, the hundreds of buildings each one contained and how each one could be used most effectively. With some 680 surplus airfields in the UK, the RAF had space to store and dispose of its unused ordnance, as well as house thousands of aircraft. Ironically, empty accommodation blocks at some sites were soon being used to rehouse Europeans displaced by a bombing campaign that had been launched from those very same airfields. Others were also hurriedly employed as 'transit centres' for German prisoners awaiting repatriation to their homeland. Many vacant bases, however, were placed into care and maintenance.

A P-51 Mustang of the 339th Fighter Group provides the backdrop for an Easter service at RAF Fowlmere in 1945. After a distinguished history, Fowlmere was vacated by the USAAF in October 1945. (Author's Collection)

In January 1946, Fowlmere, which had been vacated by the Eighth's 339th Fighter Group in October 1945, once again found itself surplus to military requirements. Having hosted the earliest American aviation units during the First World War, then witnessed the heroism of RAF No. 19 Squadron's Spitfire pilots during the Battle of Britain, Fowlmere was one of those placed on standby. It would remain empty for a further eleven years before its concrete hardstands were finally ground into aggregate and its runways torn up.

One base not immediately vacated by the Americans was Honington in Suffolk. An 'expansion period' airfield that had been opened in May 1937, Honington had then been transferred to the USAAF in June 1942 for use as an air depot for the overhaul of heavy bombers. It had also been used as a base for the 364th Fighter Group, which arrived in February 1944. When it was finally transferred back to the RAF on 26 February 1946, it was the only complete station still in use with the Eighth Air Force. Thus, when the RAF Ensign replaced the 'Stars and Stripes', Honington had been under American control longer than any other airfield in the UK.

A week after Honington's transfer, Winston Churchill (who had been replaced as Prime Minister by Clement Attlee in July 1945) visited Westminster College in Missouri, where he delivered a speech in which he uttered two now-famous phrases. The first, 'special relationship', referred to the reinforced bond between the UK and US. The second, 'Iron Curtain', drew an imaginary, but politically distinct line, between the West and several

Wing panels and B-17 fuselages litter Honington during its early use as an air depot. By the beginning of 1946, Honington remained the only active Eighth Air Force station. (Author's Collection)

Eastern European countries, which Churchill claimed had fallen under the Soviets' influence. His far-reaching speech was the cue for a major change in Allied military tack.

Two weeks later, the USAAF's Second Air Force was absorbed into the newly formed Strategic Air Command (SAC). The Eighth and Fifteenth Air Forces followed suit over the next two months. The rationale for SAC was to exercise the command and control of two of the US military's strategic nuclear strike assets: land-based strategic bombers and future Intercontinental Ballistic Missiles (ICBMs). Three days after its activation, four B-29 Superfortresses and several B-17 Flying Fortresses landed at a reconstructed Marham. They would remain on site for the next six months, trialling 'vertical bombs' (VB) fitted with guidance systems on former German U-boat pens at Kiel.

Marham had originally been a night landing ground during the First World War. In 1935, as part of the RAF's 'expansion period', construction had then begun on the airfield to accommodate a heavy bomber unit. For seven years Marham was used by the RAF to house part of its Pathfinder Force, and as a site to test rapidly advancing technology such as the aerial blind-bombing device Oboe. However, Marham was set to be revamped once again.

Shortly after the VB trials began, British Chief of the Air Staff, Sir Arthur Tedder, and Commanding General of the Army Air Forces, General Carl Spaatz, discussed the worrying

In the last week of March 1946, the first B-29 Superfortresses landed at RAF Marham, staying for the next six months. Here, a B-29 undergoes maintenance in one of its hangars. (Author's Collection)

The scale of RAF Burtonwood can be seen from this aerial image taken in August 1945. The largest airfield in Europe during the Second World War, Burtonwood was later reinstated as the USAF's preeminent UK base. (Author's Collection)

situation in Eastern Europe. They both agreed that further upgrades were needed at Marham, as well as Waddington, Lakenheath and Scampton. Doing so would allow the British to accommodate the long-range, very heavy bombers now in operation with SAC.

Burtonwood, which had retained a skeleton USAAF staff since the end of the Second World War, was also earmarked to become a supply and maintenance depot capable of supporting the bombers. In November 1946, President Harry S. Truman began allowing SAC to position portions of its fleet of B-29s closer to the USSR. Six of the aircraft duly transited through Burtonwood before flying on to Germany under the guise of a 'training deployment'.

Just over six months later, nine more B-29s landed at Marham after flying from Maryland for a goodwill visit. Publicised to add credence to SAC's 'training' programme, the visit was effectively a ruse, designed to conceal the American goal of permanently establishing a strategic air force in Europe. It was followed a month later by a joint Anglo-American announcement declaring that two groups of B-29s, totalling some sixty aircraft, would arrive in England 'for a short period of temporary duty'. Declared as being 'part of the normal long-range flight training programme' initiated over a year earlier, the two groups, consisting of 1,500 men, were to be based at both Marham and Waddington – the latter of which was a former Royal Flying Corps training station and RAF 'expansion scheme' airfield.

Under the command of General Curtis LeMay – a pioneering airman who'd seen service in both European and Pacific Theatres during the Second World War – it would be the first time that the Americans deployed combat aircraft to another sovereign state in peacetime. Yet, the USAAF was about to undergo another major change.

On 18 September 1947, following the implementation of the United States' National Security Act, the United States Air Force (USAF) was founded. Almost exactly forty years after its first antecedent, the US Army Signal Corps Aeronautical Division, had been established, the USAF now found itself completely free of the Army, Navy and Marine Corps. In quick succession, Army Air Fields were retitled 'Air Force Bases' and its personnel issued with blue uniforms and new rank insignia. A week later, Carl Spaatz was sworn in as the USAF's Chief of Staff.

By now, the USAF boasted a total strength of just over 305,000 personnel. Approximately 285 of its aircraft consisted of B-29s, which continued to use Marham for 'training purposes'. Marham would soon be joined by Lakenheath, a former RAF Bomber Command satellite to Mildenhall, which had been closed in May 1944 for reconstruction to 'very heavy bomber' standards. Lakenheath was unusual in that it was the only one of the four airfields selected by Tedder and Spaatz that hadn't been built during the RAF's 'expansion period'. Nevertheless, it re-opened in May 1948 and awaited its first American occupants.

A month later, relations between the four controlling powers in Germany worsened dramatically. The Soviet Union – in response to a German currency reform introduced by the Americans, British and French – cut the power supply to a large part of the western sector of Berlin. It was followed a day later by the blocking of road, rail and barge access through the Soviets' occupation zone of the city. The Berlin blockade would prove to be the USAF's first test as an independent fighting force.

On 26 June 1948, a total of thirty-two relief flights were carried out by the United States Air Force in Europe's (USAFE's) C-47 Skytrains, carrying milk and medicine between Wiesbaden and Berlin's Tempelhof Air Force Base. It soon became clear, however, that over 900 flights would be needed each day to sustain the two million people living in western Berlin. With only 485 aircraft at its disposal, USAFE would need all the help it could get. In support, B-29 deployments to the UK were ramped up, and with Scampton turning operational (despite a shortage of hardstands and a reduced runway length), thirty-day temporary deployments were commenced by SAC as a 'show-of-force'. The 28th Bombardment Group, with its thirty B-29s, arrived at Scampton to add much-needed strength.

Once again, outside factors were governing the need for close cooperation between the UK and US. Clement Attlee's Labour government willingly agreed to the use of British airfields by conventionally armed American bombers. Their accommodation and telecommunications were subsequently supplied free-of-charge – a perquisite never enjoyed by the USAF in any other country. The Third Air Division was quickly established at Marham to exercise control of SAC's B-29 units being deployed to the UK, while the 307th Bomb Group's Superfortresses landed at Marham and Waddington several days later. The 307th was then complemented by the 2nd Bomb Group, which arrived at Lakenheath shortly afterwards.

Away from East Anglia, Burtonwood in Lancashire saw the arrival of the first USAF technical personnel to prepare the support facilities necessary for the American deployments. Upwards of 2,500 people were eventually stationed at the airfield to operate a three-quarter-mile-long assembly line, which saw eight aircraft per day cleaned, vacuumed and hosed with detergent to continue the Berlin Airlift operation. Just as it had been the largest military airfield in Europe during the Second World War, so Burtonwood became the preeminent USAF base in the UK once again.

German civilians watch a C-54 Skymaster land at Berlin's Tempelhof airfield during the Berlin Airlift. RAF Burtonwood played its part during Operation VITTLES, operating a three-quarter-mile-long assembly line to maintain the aircraft involved in the operation. (Author's Collection)

By this time, the USAF had 466 aircraft involved in the Berlin Airlift – codenamed 'Operation VITTLES' by the Americans. Some 18,000 personnel were scattered across Europe, with approximately 6,000 being stationed in the UK. Although many had seen service during the Second World War, an intensive training programme was put into effect to familiarise the crews with the European topography. The 'temporary duty' period of the three bomb groups in England was also extended from the initial thirty-day phase to a ninety-day deployment. The Third Air Division, by now based at Bushy Park in London, was controlling the strengthening USAF presence in the UK, and it soon began negotiating American requirements for more British resources and facilities.

Unfortunately, Scampton was proving far from ideal. With its distinct lack of hardstands and insufficient runway length (3,000 feet shorter than prescribed), the airfield was deemed incapable of handling the thirty B-29s assigned to it. It was thus handed back to the RAF in January 1949.

Sculthorpe in Norfolk, on the other hand, was entirely appropriate. A former RAF Bomber Command station that had been opened in January 1943, Sculthorpe had then been closed in May 1944 to allow conversion for very heavy bombers. The Bovis construction company, using Irish labour, had originally constructed its runways, hardstands, mess facilities and accommodation in 1942. Somewhat unusually, Sculthorpe's three runways were 50 per cent longer than the average 'Class A' airfield. It was, therefore, a suitable

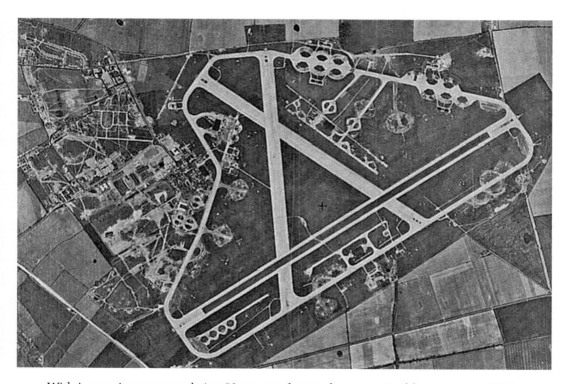

With its wartime runways being 50 per cent longer than most, Sculthorpe required little work to upgrade it for very heavy bomber operations. This aerial image shows the site in 1953. (Author's Collection)

candidate for configuration to very heavy bomber status. On 17 January 1949, the USAF's 7502nd Air Base Group duly took up position at Sculthorpe, and a month later the first B-29 of the 92nd Bomb Group landed. Fittingly, the first Eighth Air Force heavy bomb group to be formally activated during the Second World War had now returned to England.

By April 1949, a new military alliance was formed with the signing of the North Atlantic Treaty. Twelve member states, including the UK and US, formed the North Atlantic Treaty Organisation (NATO), whose aim was mutual defence in response to an attack by any external party. At the same time, the Third Air Division relocated from Bushy Park to South Ruislip – a station that would eventually employ over 1,700 people, including almost 500 British civilians. It was scheduled to become an administrative centre to coordinate USAF activities in the UK with the British Government. However, South Ruislip's opening came at an anxious time.

Due to their close proximity to the North Sea coast, the Americans became increasingly concerned that the Soviet Union could launch a surprise attack on their East Anglian bases. It was suggested that USAF units be withdrawn to airfields further west of London, behind the RAF fighter screen and anti-aircraft defences. Brize Norton, Fairford, Upper Heyford and Greenham Common were soon acquired for the purpose.

Days later, events in Germany shifted the landscape once more when the Soviet blockade of western Berlin was lifted. Some 277,000 missions had been carried out by the USAF during the Berlin Airlift. It was estimated that, on one day alone, one aircraft was landing every minute at each of western Berlin's three airfields.

By now, SAC was beginning to deploy its fleet of B-50 Superfortresses to Lakenheath, Marham and Sculthorpe. The B-50 – an upgraded version of the B-29 – was fitted with in-flight refuelling capability, enabling SAC to significantly extend its operational range. The 43rd Bomb Group, which had been based on temporary duty at Lakenheath from August 1949, held the distinction of completing the first non-stop, round-the-world flight in ninety-four hours and one minute using one of its B-50s, nicknamed *Lucky Lady II*.

During August 1949, the Soviet Union detonated its first fission bomb, leading to a hastily convened American, British and Canadian Joint Planners Conference in Washington. Specific plans for the emergency operations of RAF and USAF units based in the UK were developed. It was quickly agreed that the RAF would provide air defence of Great Britain, while the USAF would retain overall responsibility for bombing. Once again, external events were dictating an increase in American bomb groups operating from British bases.

The strengthening of SAC's presence in the UK came at a time when war broke out on the Korean Peninsula (with the crossing of the 38th Parallel into South Korea by North Korean forces). Shortly afterwards, work began on upgrading Upper Heyford in Oxfordshire for very heavy bomber use. Its main runway was extended by 2,300 feet and the number of hardstands also increased. A secure weapons store facility was also constructed. Similar work was then carried out at Fairford, as well as Brize Norton and Greenham Common.

In response to growing international tensions, other British airfields were allocated to the USAF. In June 1950, a year after RAF Bomber Command had vacated Mildenhall, US engineers arrived to begin reconstruction work. Their first task was to build a ring of anti-aircraft positions and a high-security fence. Molesworth – former home of the first American bomb unit to reach England in June 1942 (the 15th Bomb Squadron) – was also handed back to the USAF. Shortly afterwards, Molesworth's three-runway layout was overlaid with a single, more substantial runway. Bassingbourn in Cambridgeshire also found itself reinstated as an American bomber base, while Manston in Kent – an iconic RAF airfield during the Second World War – was also transferred to the Americans.

It was the latter that would have the distinction of welcoming the first permanent USAF fighter presence to the UK, when sixty-nine F-84 Thunderjets of the 20th Fighter-Bomber Wing arrived at the airfield from Langley Field, Virginia. Manston, still pockmarked with craters made by Luftwaffe bombers during the Second World War, was assigned to provide fighter escorts for the B-50s should they be used in a tactical role over Europe.

Amid the growing American presence in the UK, came problems of congestion. A number of B-50s were temporarily deployed to stations under RAF control, including Wyton and Oakington in Cambridgeshire, as well as Lindholme in Yorkshire. Several other sites were designated to become USAF support installations, including Barford St John in Oxfordshire, Chicksands in Bedfordshire and Croughton in Northamptonshire, which were all assigned as communications centres.

By the turn of 1951, a new American aircraft began arriving in the skies over the UK. On 16 January 1951, the first Convair B-36 Peacemaker touched down at Lakenheath for a series of training exercises with RAF Fighter Command. Its unique design included ten engines, comprising six radial propellers and four jet engines – more than any other mass-produced aircraft at the time. The aircraft's impressive wingspan of 230 feet dwarfed the RAF fighter jets that escorted it into Lakenheath.

The scale of the ten-engine B-36 Peacemaker can clearly be seen in this image taken at Lakenheath on 17 January 1951. The 7th Bomb Group's aircraft had arrived for a series of training exercises. (Author's Collection)

In the early 1950s, RAF Prestwick was upgraded to cope with the increasing volume of transport aircraft crossing the Atlantic. General Dwight D. Eisenhower is pictured being greeted at Prestwick in 1952 – the same year he ran for the US presidency. (Author's Collection)

The following month, the British and American governments agreed to a special airfield construction programme costing in excess of $100 million. Several additional Second World War airfields were also to be reconstructed to accommodate the new jet aircraft now being produced. The agreement covered twenty-three bases, which would be used for strategic and tactical purposes, while three air depots would provide logistical support. The increased volume of aircraft now flying between the US and UK also saw Prestwick reactivated as a Military Air Transport Service hub. To cope with the growing number of arrivals, its main runway was extended, hardstanding increased and a new terminal constructed. The adjacent RAF Ayr was also reopened as a storage site.

All this came at a time when American forces in the UK were being reorganised to allow better control of their growing strength. SAC activated the 7th Air Division at South Ruislip to control its deployed bomber units, while the Third Air Division was inactivated and replaced by the Third Air Force, also headquartered at South Ruislip. The Third Air Force now came under the control of USAFE and was tasked with receiving tactical units into the UK and providing tactical support to the USAF and other American units in the country.

The 7th Air Division would ultimately control fifteen SAC-allocated bases in the UK – Bassingbourn, Brize Norton, Carnaby, Fairford, Greenham Common, Lakenheath, Lindholme, Manston, Marham, Mildenhall, Sculthorpe, Upper Heyford, Waddington,

Woodbridge and Wyton. Its ultimate mission was to support 'TROJAN' – the codename for a plan to retaliate if the Soviet Union waged war.

The build-up of the USAF in the UK continued into March 1951 with the transfer of Bentwaters and Shepherds Grove, both in Suffolk. Before either could accommodate the planned arrival of American jet fighters, work was required to bring both airfields up to NATO standards. Over the next five months, construction was completed on their operational and support facilities. The upgrades came at a time when the USAF began the steady transfer of thirteen combat wings from the US to USAFE, numbering some 800 aircraft and 18,000 personnel. Four of the wings were scheduled for deployment to the UK.

The following month, an extensive reconstruction project began at Greenham Common. Previously used by the Ninth Air Force during the Second World War, its original three-runway layout and twenty-seven hardstands (plus twenty-five loops) were almost entirely ripped up, allowing American engineers to construct a new 10,000-foot runway, parallel taxiways and an extensive area of hardstandings. During Greenham Common's overhaul, several houses and two pubs were demolished to make way for a new technical and domestic site. Nevertheless, it would be almost three years before refurbishment was completed and the first flying unit arrived.

An aerial shot of Greenham Common taken sometime in 1944. The airfield's layout would significantly change during the 1950s, when its three runways were replaced by a single 10,000-foot runway. (Author's Collection)

A Fairchild C-119 Flying Boxcar pictured at RAF Bovingdon during an open day in the 1950s. This unusual twin-boom aircraft was used for the transportation of cargo, personnel and equipment. (Author's Collection)

RAF Bovingdon, an airfield that had been a valuable asset to the Eighth Air Force Headquarters during the Second World War, once again found itself perfectly located for reallocation. Thanks to its post-war use as a civilian airport, and its close proximity to the USAF's Third Air Force Headquarters at South Ruislip, the Americans returned on 25 May 1951 to establish a base for their C-47 transporters. It would remain a USAF installation for the next eleven years.

Another British airfield welcomed back into the American fold was Wethersfield in Essex – a former Ninth Air Force base. It was initially assigned to the Third Air Force as a USAF installation on 24 August 1951. However, it would be a further nine months before the first American aircraft touched down. Shepherds Grove, on the other hand – an airfield that had been transferred to the USAAF during the Second World War, but never used – saw the arrival of the first F-86 Sabres in the UK three days later. Their appearance was followed a fortnight later by further F-86 arrivals at Bentwaters. It was a significant boost for the air defence of Great Britain.

RAF Upper Heyford became the first of the 'midland' group of SAC bases to reopen after its extensive renovation, when the first of fifteen B-50Ds arrived in December 1951. Another facility to reopen, although not following any reconstruction, was 'Pinetree', the former Eighth Air Force Headquarters at Wycombe Abbey. Disused since the end of the Second World War, its underground bunker was reoccupied by elements of the 7th Air Division in May 1952. Five months later, Chelveston, one of the earliest airfields to be

Wethersfield saw the return of the Americans in May 1952. With many of its wartime buildings still in place (including a Nissen hut that eventually served as a barber shop), Wethersfield would remain a USAF base for almost forty years. (Author's Collection)

assigned to the Eighth Air Force in March 1942, was also in line for reopening. Significant work would be carried out, one element being a new 12,000-foot runway – the longest in the UK. However, Chelveston would never regain the elevated status it enjoyed as the pioneering heavy bomber airfield it once was during the Second World War.

With scores of airfields being reinstated, congestion quickly became a problem. In June 1952, elements of the 20th Fighter-Bomber Wing were compelled to leave Wethersfield due to its restricted space. Some F-84s had initially been moved to Bentwaters in Suffolk. However, when Woodbridge reopened in October 1952, the F-84s found themselves in the air yet again – this time for the short 3-mile hop from Bentwaters.

By now, Brize Norton had joined other reconstructed 'midland' bases that had been formally transferred. Used largely as a training airfield during the Second World War, Brize Norton was soon accommodating temporary duty SAC elements. However, it was Fairford that would capture the biggest prize of all.

On 7 April 1954, two B-47 Stratojets of the 306th Bomb Wing began their approach into the Gloucestershire airfield. Developed at the end of the Second World War, the SAC's latest asset was fitted with six turbojets in underwing pods. These upgraded engines had enabled both B-47s to cross the Atlantic from Maine to Fairford in just five hours and thirty-eight minutes. Approaching Fairford, their undercarriages were lowered and the aircraft descended by 20,000 feet in four minutes. On touchdown, they became the first B-47s to land in Britain after a record-breaking flight.

Thus began a period of B-47 duty postings to the UK that involved an entire wing of forty-five aircraft (plus around twenty KC-97 Stratofreighter fuel tankers) being held at readiness for ninety days at bases such as Fairford. After the 'temporary duty' period was

43

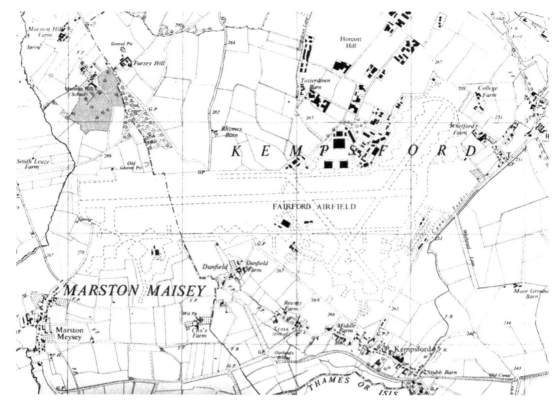

RAF Fairford welcomed the first B-47 Stratojets to the UK in April 1954. They used 7,000 feet of its main runway before stopping. Fairford's infrastructure is shown here overlaid on a 1960s Ordnance Survey map. (Airfield Research Group)

up, another wing arrived from a different airfield. Records would also continue to be set. On 28 July 1953, a day after the Korean War ended, two more B-47s flew from Goose Air Base in Newfoundland to Fairford in just four hours and fourteen minutes. The USAF was now routinely flexing its wings.

By November 1953, Burtonwood was home to a squadron of Superfortresses tasked with collecting weather data in order to provide forecasts to both the US Military Air Transport Services (MATS) and US Weather Bureau. The weather the crews experienced in the north of England was significantly different from their previous base in Bermuda. However, now equipped with its own school and shop, and housing many American airmen, Burtonwood was expanding once again. When its buildings were paid for with American tobacco profits, they became colloquially known as 'Tobacco Houses'.

Other British airfields also began to receive USAF aircraft capable of varying roles. Following the extension of its main runway and the addition of more modern facilities, Molesworth saw its first aircraft land in February 1954 after an eight-year absence. A number of B-29 Superfortresses arrived to begin preparing for the task of rescuing American crews should they be shot down over enemy territory. Tactical reconnaissance squadrons also arrived at Sculthorpe, while fighter-interceptors were

Following extensive reconstruction in the 1950s, including the building of a new 9,000-foot runway, Molesworth saw American aircraft finally return in 1954. (Author's Collection)

reassigned to Manston. The USAF could now call upon nine airfields, from Manston in the far south-east to Burtonwood in the north-west.

Towards the end of 1955, other conflicts began to draw more American aircraft to the UK. The US Military Assistance Advisory Group (MAAG) had been deployed to Southeast Asia by President Truman to assist the French military in their struggle with the Viet Minh. On 1 November 1955, MAAG Vietnam was established, officially heralding the start of the Vietnam War. The following year, Soviet troops invaded Hungary to quell a civilian uprising. It prompted the USAF to divert more bombers to the UK. Burtonwood welcomed eleven B-36s, while sixteen landed at Greenham Common. Other British airfields also saw an increase in B-47 deployments.

By now, American bombers were increasingly being equipped with nuclear capability. On 27 July 1956, one B-47 caused a near catastrophe at Lakenheath when it crashed into a storage igloo, killing all four crewmen. The aircraft was carrying three nuclear weapons and 8,000 lb of high explosives. Fortunately, none of them exploded. However, the narrow escape served to highlight the dangers being faced by those in the air, and an unwitting British public on the ground.

RAF Bruntingthorpe in Leicestershire joined the growing list of USAF in bases in the UK when it was activated by SAC on 1 March 1957. Opened fifteen years earlier as an RAF Bomber Command training base, the airfield had been reconstructed with a new 10,000-foot runway. Despite being immediately designated as a satellite airfield for Alconbury, Bruntingthorpe would have to wait two years before its first aircraft landed.

In 1958, SAC decided that its ninety-day temporary duty postings would be replaced by a new system called 'Reflex'. The change would consist of three-week deployments involving a number of aircraft from different bomb wings, rather than one entire bomb wing. 'Reflex' would allow SAC to group a number of aircraft from several US bases at one British airfield in order to maintain a more permanent presence. Greenham Common and Fairford saw the first deployments, with five bomb wings despatching their B-47s from the US in early January. The move was a blessing in disguise for the British public, as the bombers only flew on 'Reflex Alert', meaning that much of their time was spent on the ground.

By this time, Manston was deemed surplus to British air defence requirements. Its resident fighter-interceptor wing was reassigned to West Germany and the airfield was soon returned to the RAF. Shepherds Grove suffered a similar fate when it, too, was released from USAF control. Having received the first F-86 Sabres to be based in Britain (thus becoming the first foreign aircraft to be assigned to the air defence of the UK), the airfield was relinquished to RAF Bomber Command in December. The airfield's resident USAF fighters – F-84 Thunderstreaks – were duly moved to both Woodbridge and Wethersfield. Nevertheless, some of the domestic sites were retained by the USAF and continued to be used as married quarters for personnel based at Lakenheath.

RAF Burtonwood was also experiencing a drawdown. In March 1959, the USAF's Military Air Transport Service was relocated from the Lancashire airfield to Suffolk's Mildenhall. Burtonwood's flightline was subsequently closed in April, although the depot continued to be used as a storage facility for US weapons. Mildenhall, however, was undergoing yet another renaissance.

SAC had determined that the airfield's runways were no longer suitable for its newer aircraft and it was handed over to the USAF. As a result, all operational decisions regarding the USAF in the UK would subsequently be made from Mildenhall. The airfield was also set to become 'the Gateway to the UK' after the opening of the USAF's main passenger terminal in Great Britain.

In June 1959, as a result of a new defence policy, French President Charles De Gaulle began prohibiting NATO nuclear weapons from being stationed in France. The decision sparked a series of USAFE redeployments to the UK and a change in jurisdiction for a number of British airfields. In particular, Alconbury, Bruntingthorpe and Chelveston were all transferred from SAC to USAFE. Together with Molesworth, these four airfields evolved into a four-base complex that would eventually provide electronic and photographic reconnaissance missions.

One of the American units forced to redeploy from France – the 48th Tactical Fighter Wing – had enjoyed an especially close relationship with the citizens of a small commune close to its Chaumont-Semoutiers Air Force Base. Prior to De Gaulle's decision, the people of Chaumont had petitioned to have the unit named the 'Statue of Liberty Wing' in honour of its exploits over France as a fighter group during the Second World War. Thanks to this

A Douglas C-124 Globemaster II takes on its cargo of personnel during an exercise at Mildenhall in the mid-1960s. As the USAF's main passenger terminal, Mildenhall effectively became the 'Gateway to the UK'. (Author's Collection)

entente cordiale, the 48th duly became the only USAF unit to receive both a numeric and descriptive designation – one it still holds today as it continues flying from Lakenheath, the UK base it first arrived at in 1960.

The first F-100 Super Sabres of the 48th began landing at the Suffolk airfield on 15 January, and the deployment quickly placed the airfield's infrastructure under strain. To cope with the increase in base population, a massive expansion then followed. A new theatre, junior high school and forty-five brick housing units were constructed within eighteen months. A large base hospital then followed, subsequently becoming the primary medical facility for American forces in the UK.

Despite the goodwill shown by the people of France, the physical form of Churchill's 'Iron Curtain' appeared overnight in Germany on 12 August 1961. The Soviet-backed East German Government began erecting the Berlin Wall to stem an exodus of Germans leaving its eastern sector. In response, US President John F. Kennedy's administration began rapidly increasing American tactical air power in Europe. A two-phase deployment to Europe eventually saw the largest overseas movement of American aircraft since the Second World War.

The enormous B-52 Stratofortress – an aircraft that had previously visited the UK only rarely – was soon making periodic flights to Greenham Common and Fairford. Despite local fears that there would be an influx of the huge bombers, the B-52 would never be based in the UK. It was, however, used with increasing frequency, although only for temporary deployments or training exercises.

By March 1962, both Bruntingthorpe and Chelveston were closed to flying when their resident tactical reconnaissance units moved to France. The latter would subsequently become a USAF communication and storage centre, while the former saw most of its infrastructure either demolished or sold off. Later that same year, Bovingdon was handed back to the RAF when its USAF lodger unit transferred to Mildenhall. All this came at a time when the Soviet Union was secretly deploying nuclear missiles to Cuba. The shock discovery led to the placement of American forces on global high alert. As a result, nuclear-capable F-100 Super Sabre tactical fighter-bombers were readied at Wethersfield and Lakenheath as part of a coordinated strategy with RAF-manned Thor missiles. Fortunately, the withdrawal of the Soviet Union's missiles from Cuba averted this most serious of crises.

By now, the ageing B-47 Stratojet was being replaced by the more-advanced Convair B-58 Hustler – the first supersonic bomber to enter service with the USAF. A number of B-58s visited Brize Norton and Greenham Common following the Cuban Missile Crisis, one of which broke a world record flying from Tokyo to the UK in just eight hours and thirty-five minutes. However, despite global tensions, SAC's role in the UK was drawing to a close. In the summer of 1964, both Fairford and Greenham Common finished supporting 'Reflex Alerts' and reverted to Ministry of Defence (MoD) control. A 10 per cent reduction in USAF personnel then followed as the B-47s and their supporting tanker aircraft were withdrawn from the UK. The last Stratojet departed Brize Norton on 1 April 1965 and the Oxfordshire airfield found itself back under MoD control with the termination of SAC bomber operations in Britain. Nevertheless, another change in policy across the English Channel would swell the USAF's presence in the UK once again.

CHAPTER THREE

An Essential Relationship

With the departure of SAC, all but one of the four 'midland' bases remained in American hands. Upper Heyford was transferred to the USAF and became an advanced base for a detachment of reconnaissance aircraft supporting strategic wings operating out of Alaska and Spain. Upper Heyford would subsequently host a wide range of aircraft. Yet the diversity of aircraft types in the USAF arsenal also posed a significant and growing maintenance challenge.

One aircraft that could perform a wide variety of roles (air defence, ground support and aerial reconnaissance) and would solve the issue of standardisation, was the McDonnell

On 12 May 1965, the first F-4 Phantoms arrived in the UK, pictured here on the ramp at Alconbury. Other Phantoms also arrived at Bentwaters and Woodbridge. (Author's Collection)

F-4 Phantom – the USAF's first all-weather, day and night tactical reconnaissance aircraft. On 12 May 1965, two Phantoms touched down at Alconbury after a non-stop flight from North Carolina. They were the first F-4s to land in the UK, and were soon followed by further arrivals at Bentwaters and Woodbridge. Although it would be another twenty years before American Phantoms departed the UK for good, the USAF was soon facing another logistical headache.

On 7 March 1965, French President Charles de Gaulle delivered a letter to the heads of five governments, including those of America and Britain. It contained a bombshell:

> ... France proposes to recover the entire exercise of her sovereignty over her territory, presently impaired by the permanent presence of allied military elements or by constant utilization which is made of her air space, to terminate her participation in the 'integrated' commands and no longer places her forces at the disposal of NATO ...

As a result, the Allies were given just one year to remove all troops and material from French territory. The move drew a stinging response from US President Lyndon Johnson, who asked de Gaulle if the demand included the exhumation of his country's war dead. With a considerable concentration of American air power in Northern France, the loss of the bases was a painful blow. Some 33,000 personnel and their families, as well as all aircraft and equipment belonging to eleven tactical units and four interceptor squadrons, had to be relocated to West Germany, the Netherlands and Great Britain. 'Operation FRELOC' (Fast Relocation) was duly put into effect in the summer of 1966.

RAF Burtonwood, which had been operating as a reserve USAF base, quickly became a receiving depot for American military hardware being withdrawn from France. Under US Army control, its main warehouse – reputedly the largest building under a single roof in Europe – was soon heaving under a growing mountain of supplies.

Approximately 8,000 USAF personnel and their families began the transfer to Britain as part of 'Operation FRELOC'. The upheaval, although inconvenient, was viewed optimistically by some: 'It is sad that the French take this attitude', declared one US airman. 'I think that most of us feel this way. But Britain is regarded as a better posting – I mean to say, [the English] speak American, so it's easier.'

Over the next few months, both Upper Heyford and Mildenhall received tactical reconnaissance and troop carrier wings from redundant bases in France. Chelveston, Molesworth and Sculthorpe were all designated to be storage sites, while Feltwell in Norfolk was allocated as a housing annexe for the burgeoning population at Mildenhall. By early January 1967, even Greenham Common, which had been closed to flying following the departure of SAC, found itself reopened to handle an increasing flow of personnel and equipment from French bases.

The last USAF aircraft to depart France took off on 31 May 1967. With the completion of 'FRELOC', the USAF's offensive presence in Britain had expanded significantly. It had also evolved into one of a purely tactical nature. F-4 Phantoms continued to arrive in the UK, while Lockheed C-130 Hercules and heavy-duty Sikorsky HH-53 Jolly Green Giant helicopters moved to Woodbridge for air-sea rescue duties. Upper Heyford, on the other hand, was undergoing extensive modifications in preparation for the arrival of a brand-new type of aircraft.

On 12 September 1970, two swing-wing General Dynamics F-111 Aardvarks touched down at the Oxfordshire base – the first of seventy-two assigned to the 20th Tactical Fighter Wing (20th TFW), which had recently relocated from Wethersfield in Essex. The F-111s were replacements for the 20th TFW's North American F-100 Super Sabres, and conversion was due to be carried out at Upper Heyford. Although it would be another year before the crews would be operationally ready, the F-111 became a familiar sight, flying at 8 miles per minute 500 feet above the Oxfordshire countryside.

Upper Heyford's development continued into 1972. Two maintenance hangars and extensive housing for its officers were built, followed a year later by the construction of new storage sheds, a bowling alley and shopping centre, plus the renovation of its airmen's dormitories. It was a similar story at Mildenhall and Woodbridge, where forty-eight single officers' quarters and an American high school were built respectively. Somewhat ironically, however, High Wycombe's 'Pinetree' was abandoned by the USAF at the same time and turned over to the London Central Elementary High School for American children. It has since returned to its pre-war status as a private girls' school.

When the Third Air Force headquarters was transferred to Mildenhall, South Ruislip, which had been opened in 1949, found itself surplus to USAF requirements. As a result, seventy-seven civilian members of staff were made redundant and its buildings left empty. For a brief period between 1977 and 1978, the site was used as a film location for the British television drama *Z Cars*, before being demolished in 1995.

In September 1970, Upper Heyford welcomed the first two F-111 Aardvarks to the UK. They would become a familiar sight, flying at low-level over the Oxfordshire countryside. (Author's Collection)

By the autumn of 1972, a review of defence land holdings took place. The 'Nugent Report' concluded that of the 662,000 acres of defence land, a total of 32,700 acres should be released. The report suggested that ninety-seven sites would be affected, including land occupied by airfields. Molesworth was the first to feel the impact, being closed to flying within a year. Nevertheless, it continued serving as an education and housing centre, and saw its controversial return to operational use in the 1980s.

Despite the 'Nugent Report', the principal USAF bases in the UK continued highlighting their importance. In October 1972, Egypt and Syria invaded Israel sparking the Yom Kippur War. The USAF was quickly placed on high alert. Its potential Order of Battle from the UK involved F-4 Phantoms at Alconbury and Bentwaters, F-111s at Lakenheath and Upper Heyford and C-130 Hercules at Woodbridge and Mildenhall – the latter being used to ferry spares and equipment to the fighter-bomber bases. After nineteen days, a ceasefire was brokered and the threat subsided.

By 1976, Mildenhall was beginning to host rotational operations of the Lockheed U-2 and SR-71 Blackbird aircraft – both used to carry out strategic photo reconnaissance missions as part of the first Strategic Arms Limitation Talks (SALT-1). With the US and Soviet Union agreeing to a partial freeze on the number of nuclear weapons, both aircraft types were used to ensure that the Soviets were observing their part of the agreement. However, by the following year the number of tactical reconnaissance aircraft being used in the UK dwindled amid budget cuts and the advent of reconnaissance satellites.

In October 1972, the Yom Kippur War erupted in the Middle East. Elements from several UK bases were placed on high alert, including the C-130 Hercules of the 67th Air Rescue Squadron based at Woodbridge. (Robin A. Walker)

An SR-71 of Detachment 4 of the 9th Strategic Reconnaissance Wing being readied at Mildenhall in April 1976. The aircraft was used to monitor Soviet activities following the SALT-1 agreement. (Terry Senior)

Alconbury was one airfield that saw several of its reconnaissance squadrons deactivated. Nevertheless, it also witnessed the activation of a new unit that was tasked with providing combat tactics training for other NATO countries in Europe. The 527th Tactical Fighter Aggressor Squadron duly welcomed the first of its new Northrop F-5 Tiger jets on 21 May 1976 and was declared fully operational seven months later.

By the spring of 1977, the USAF announced plans to reactivate Greenham Common as a base for its expanding European Tanker Task Force. Up to twenty Boeing KC-135 Stratotanker aircraft required a new base due to a lack of capacity at Mildenhall. Greenham Common had the necessary facilities to accommodate the aircraft, but a huge public outcry followed. Derived from the Boeing 707 airliner, the KC-135 was much noisier and required a significantly longer take-off run and shallow climb-out. Extensive research by protestors found that potential noise levels would be close to the threshold of pain. The plan was subsequently vetoed by the British Defence Secretary, Fred Mulley. Despite the decision, however, Fairford and Brize Norton were proposed as viable alternatives. The latter was still active with the RAF, while the former had been vacated in 1971. Protests spread to both bases, but after a series of noise tests Fairford was accepted as 'the only suitable base in the short term'. Subsequently, Stratotankers from Spain and Greece made regular appearances over the Cotswolds.

Just over a year later, further KC-135s transferred from Germany to Mildenhall. The 306th Strategic Wing, part of SAC, arrived at the airfield on 1 July 1978.

Greenham Common suffered the first of its protests in 1977 when it was announced as the base for the European Tanker Task Force. The KC-135 – derived from the Boeing 707 – was found to be too noisy and the aircraft were soon redirected to Fairford. (Author's Collection)

Operating a mix of air refuelling and reconnaissance types, the 306th became a focal point for all SAC operations in Europe, with Mildenhall becoming SAC's European reconnaissance centre.

Bentwaters was also enjoying time in the limelight. The Suffolk airfield welcomed a new type of aircraft in January 1979, when the Fairchild A-10 Thunderbolt arrived to begin work as a ground attack and close support aircraft. Operating with the 81st Tactical Fighter Wing (81st TFW), the A-10 was deployed from Bentwaters and nearby Woodbridge to Forward Operating Locations (FOLs) in West Germany.

With the expansion of British bases and the opening of numerous FOLs, the British and American governments agreed that a new engineering unit should be deployed to the UK to provide rapid runway repairs. The main Rapid Engineer Deployable Heavy Operational Repair Squadron Engineers (RED HORSE) unit was the 819th Civil Engineering Squadron, which had seen service in Vietnam. In December 1978, the 819th moved from Kansas to Wethersfield in Essex, where it would remain until 1990.

The 819th's arrival coincided with the reconstruction of a number of USAF bases in the UK. Mildenhall saw the initiation of improved airfield lighting, new revetments for the protection of its aircraft, and extensive housing schemes. Upper Heyford received a new parallel taxi-track and improved medical facilities, while Greenham Common saw its runway, aprons and hardstands reinforced. More importantly, however, the latter also received preparatory work for the arrival of a controversial new type of weapon.

On 12 December 1978, NATO agreed to deploy 572 new nuclear missiles around Europe. The majority of the weapons would be Ground-Launched Cruise Missiles (GLCM) operated by the USAF, with 160 based in the UK. Both Greenham Common and a reactivated Molesworth were selected to house the missiles, all stored in special grass-covered bunkers. The British Government also agreed to contribute over 200 Armed Forces personnel for security purposes.

In June 1980, it was publicly announced that Greenham Common would become the first site to receive the new weapons. The announcement was greeted with uproar by the Campaign for Nuclear Disarmament (CND). In September the following year, the Greenham Common Women's Peace Camp was established outside the base, when a Welsh group (Women for Life on Earth) arrived to protest. Similar peace camps were set up at other bases around the country. Blockades of Greenham Common then followed when the 501st Tactical Missile Wing arrived at its new base. Several weeks later, an estimated

In 1978, the 819th Civil Engineering Squadron moved from Kansas to Wethersfield. Dubbed 'RED HORSE', its engineers were deployed to provide rapid runway repairs.
(Kim Steiner)

In December 1982, an estimated 30,000 women held hands around Greenham Common's perimeter in protest at the siting of nuclear missiles. Their 'Peace Camp' would remain in place for almost twenty years. (Author's Collection)

30,000 women held hands around the airfield's 6-mile perimeter in protest. Nevertheless, the demonstrations failed to prevent a C-141 Starlifter from delivering the first GLCMs to Greenham Common on 14 November 1983. It would be some time before the missiles were permanently removed from British bases. Before then, however, the USAF would be tasked with delivering a more conventional weapon in equally trying circumstances.

An escalating confrontation between the United States and Libya came to a head in December 1985 when a number of terrorist attacks in Rome and Vienna killed five American citizens. It was the catalyst for 'Operation EL DORADO CANYON' – a series of air strikes against Libya by the United States.

In the afternoon of 14 April 1986, twenty-eight McDonnell Douglas KC-10 refuelling tankers began taking off from Mildenhall and Fairford, forming the largest armada of refuelling aircraft ever seen over Europe. Their task was a necessary one after the French, Spanish and Italian governments all refused overflight permission for the USAF's Libyan strike force. As a result, the fifteen F-111s that left Lakenheath thirty-five minutes later (backed up by electronic countermeasures aircraft from Upper Heyford) were forced to fly a circuitous 2,800-nautical-mile route around the coasts of France and Spain. With a payload of 6,000 lb and a combat radius of 1,100 nautical miles, the F-111s required three refuelling contacts before turning in for Libya.

The F-111s' targets included the military side of Tripoli Airport, as well as a soldiers' barracks in the city and a port facility 10 miles to the west. Flying at low level, the aircraft were joined by jets from the US Navy's Sixth Fleet, which was positioned in the Gulf of Sirte. In an attack lasting roughly eight minutes, one F-111 was shot down with the loss of its two crew members. At dawn on 15 April, the remaining F-111s began landing back at Lakenheath.

'EL DORADO CANYON' was the first time that that USAF's Third Air Force had been used in anger from the UK. Public reaction swung between dismay (that US forces in the UK could be used for unilateral action) and anger (that British bases had been used for the purpose). The CND subsequently organised large demonstrations at Lakenheath,

56

Mildenhall, Upper Heyford and Fairford, but the protests soon dissipated. Nevertheless, there was a growing realisation that USAF bases in the UK, and their local communities, could soon become prime targets for terrorist attack. For the Americans at Lakenheath, however, the raid gave rise to the acronym LIBYA – 'Lakenheath is bombing your ass'.

Later that same year, during a meeting in Reykjavík, Iceland, US President Ronald Reagan and his Soviet counterpart, Mikhail Gorbachev, agreed in principle to remove Intermediate-Range Nuclear Forces from Europe. Their meeting came just two months before the first GLCMs arrived at Molesworth – the other UK base selected to house the missiles. The Intermediate-Range Nuclear Forces Treaty would be ratified the following year, and the missiles would be removed from both Molesworth and Greenham Common by 1991.

During the late 1980s, work was carried out at both Alconbury and Mildenhall to resurface their ageing runways. Tenants from both bases were relocated to Sculthorpe and Wyton while the resurfacing work took place. However, between the fall of the Berlin Wall in November 1989 and the collapse of the Soviet Union two years later, Sculthorpe, Bentwaters, Woodbridge, Chicksands, Greenham Common, Wethersfield and Upper Heyford were all earmarked for closure. Nevertheless, events in the Middle East would alter the British landscape once again.

On 2 August 1990, the Iraqi Army invaded Kuwait, triggering 'Operation DESERT SHIELD'. Mildenhall's new runway immediately saw a dramatic increase in movements as numerous tankers and transporters transited through on their way to the Middle East. Fairford found itself reactivated once again in order to receive B-52 bombers from the US, while Lakenheath, Upper Heyford and Woodbridge deployed units to Turkey and Saudi Arabia.

On 17 January 1991, 'Operation DESERT STORM' was put into effect. Two weeks later, the first of ten B-52s landed at Fairford. Within a matter of days, the first fully loaded B-52

B-52 *What's Up Doc?* of the 806th Bomb Wing awaits its next mission from Fairford during 'Operation DESERT STORM'. A total of sixty sorties were carried out from the airfield over a two-week period. (Stuart Freer)

took off from the airfield to strike Iraqi Republican Guard units dug in around Kuwait. A further fifty-nine sorties then followed over a two-week period, in which 1,158 tons of bombs were dropped.

After the removal of Iraqi forces from Kuwait and the return of UK-based USAF aircraft, a drawdown of US forces in Britain slowly took place. The A-10s of the 10th Tactical Fighter Wing departed Alconbury for the USA, followed by those of the 81st TFW at Bentwaters. A change in tenancy then took place at Mildenhall, when the 100th Air Refuelling Wing (100th ARW) arrived to become the host unit and headquarters of the European Tanker Task Force. Lakenheath also witnessed a new arrival in the form of the McDonnell Douglas F-15 Strike Eagle – an aircraft that had performed solidly during the Gulf War after seeking and destroying Iraqi Scud missiles at night.

The reorganisation of US forces in the UK coincided with a redirection of the USAF as a whole. Strategic Air Command, Tactical Air Command and Military Air Command were all inactivated on 1 June 1992 and replaced by Air Combat Command (operating fighters, bombers and missiles) and Air Mobility Command (operating tankers and transporters). The changes had little effect on bases such as Greenham Common, which was returned to the British MoD on 11 September 1992. Almost exactly five months later, Greenham Common, which had housed the first cruise missiles, and enjoyed an on-off association with American military aviation for almost fifty years, was declared surplus to requirement. The only stalwarts of the airfield were the peace camps, which remained in place until 2000 to ensure the base was closed and its land returned to the public.

A similar fate befell Woodbridge. Just weeks after US President Bill Clinton attended a ceremony in Berlin marking the inactivation of US land and air forces in the German city,

An F-15 Strike Eagle of the 48th FW ('Liberty Wing') outside its Hardened Aircraft Shelter at Lakenheath. The first F-15 arrived at the airfield in December 1992. (Richard E. Flagg)

the Suffolk airfield, which had proved so life-saving during the Second World War, was closed with the departure of its last A-10 Thunderbolt. Four months later, Upper Heyford followed suit when its flight line was closed after the 55th Fighter Squadron's aircraft departed for the US. Nevertheless, the squadron left a memento in the form of one of its F-111s, which remains on display in the American Air Museum at Duxford.

In March 1995, after much of Alconbury had been returned to the British MoD, its last Hercules transporters and Sikorsky MH-53 helicopters lifted off for the short flight to Mildenhall. The partial closure of Alconbury had a direct effect on Upwood in Cambridgeshire, which had housed many of Alconbury's airmen since 1981. With the need for housing no longer necessary, Upwood was returned to the British Government in September 1995.

Following the World Trade Center and Pentagon terrorist attacks on 11 September 2001, Lakenheath's 48th Fighter Wing – also known as the 'Liberty Wing' – played a pivotal role in Operations 'ENDURING FREEDOM – AFGHANISTAN' and 'IRAQI FREEDOM'. During the latter, neighbouring Mildenhall also played its part when elements of the 491st Air Expeditionary Group operated from the base using Lockheed C-141 Starlifters – eighteen of which were on the ground at Mildenhall at the same time.

In March 2005, an additional non-flying USAF facility was opened at Digby in Lincolnshire. A former Royal Naval Air Service flying site during the First World War and the RAF's oldest operational station, Digby then began hosting operations for the MoD's Joint Service Signals Organisation – a tri-services signals installation shared by members of the three services of both the British and American Armed Forces.

RAF Digby's station headquarters, pictured in 2017. The RAF's oldest operational station has been home to a tri-service signals organisation from both the British and American Armed Forces since 2005. (Richard E. Flagg)

Blenheim Crescent in London was transferred to the USAF in 2006. Initially used by the US Navy, the facility is now home to a post office, which serves American personnel stationed in London. (Master Sgt. John Barton)

Eighteen months later, the USAF moved into another non-flying facility at Blenheim Crescent, London. Originally on lease to the US Navy, Blenheim Crescent was transferred to the USAF on 1 October. RAF Croughton's 422nd Air Base Group assumed administrative duties for the base, which was responsible in itself for the administration of American forces in the UK.

However, the history of the USAF's former bases could not be forgotten. In 2011, almost exactly fifty years after the Cuban Missile Crisis, Harrington's Thor missile site was given Grade II listed status. Although operated by the RAF at the time of the crisis, Harrington's association with the USAF at a time of heightened tensions was emphasised when the then Chief Executive of English Heritage, Dr Simon Thurley, remarked: 'Our Cold War heritage is a complicated and not always easily loved collection of concrete bunkers and silos. But they are the castles and forts of the twentieth century.'

The Cold War was also on the minds of Prime Minister David Cameron and President Barack Obama, when the latter made a state visit to the UK in May 2011. In a joint article written for *The Times*, both men paid tribute to the 'special relationship', deeming it to be much more significant:

> ... the Cold War reached [its] conclusion because of the actions of many brave individuals and many strong nations, but we saw how the bond between our two countries – and our two leaders at the time – proved such a vital catalyst for change ... ours is not just a special relationship, it is an essential relationship – for us and for the world.

One year later, USAFE was re-designated USAFE-AFAFRICA (United States Air Force – Air Forces Africa). The organisation could trace its lineage back to 1 February 1942, when it was activated as the Eighth Air Force of the USAAF. Although headquartered in Germany, USAFE-AFAFRICA still consists of seven main operating bases, two of which are Lakenheath and Mildenhall, as well as another 114 'geographically separated locations'.

An aerial view of Harrington's Thor missile site. The area was given Grade II listed status in 2011 by English Heritage, who described the storage buildings as 'the castles and forts of the twentieth century'. (Martyn Jones)

In 2014, 'Operation INHERENT RESOLVE' (a military intervention against the Islamic State of Iraq and Syria) drew elements of Lakenheath and Mildenhall to the Middle East. Deployments of KC-135 tankers from the former supported F-15E Strike Eagle fighter-bombers from the latter, both operating from Incirlik Air Base in Turkey. By the end of 2015, Lakenheath's 48th FW had contributed to some 15,000 airstrikes in the region.

Sadly, despite Mildenhall's almost constant American presence since the Second World War, the USAF announced that it would be leaving the airfield in order to save £500 million a year across Europe. Approximately 2,600 personnel were expected be moved to other USAF locations in the UK and Germany. The closure would also come at a cost of £200 million a year to the Suffolk economy. At the same time, the UK MoD announced that activities at Molesworth and Alconbury would also be consolidated at Croughton in Northamptonshire. Nevertheless, in September 2017 the USAF made a further announcement stating that all three bases would remain operational until at least 2024. Delays to 'project design and construction for the move of assets from RAF Mildenhall' were cited as the reason for postponement.

The end may be in sight for some, but for many others their extraordinary pasts are becoming increasingly difficult to see.

CHAPTER FOUR

How the Land Lies

Just a handful of the 200 or so airfields used at one time or another by antecedents of the USAF have survived the ravages of time. Many have gradually faded into the landscape, while others have seen various uses from film sets to turkey farms. Around a dozen are still in operational use with the USAF today.

1. Upwood

One of the last USAF airfields to be returned to the British Government was RAF Upwood in Cambridgeshire. Still containing a medical complex and housing area, it was finally closed in 2012. The following year, its disused medical wing was demolished to make way for private housing. However, following the site's complete closure in 2013, many of this former First World War airfield's buildings were vandalised by those with little understanding of its rich and varied history. It is a scourge not uncommon at many disused airfields today.

A depressing image of RAF Upwood's Guardroom taken in 2018. Since its complete closure in 2013, this former First World War airfield has attracted those with little appreciation of its history. (Richard E. Flagg)

An aerial view of RAF Upper Heyford taken in 2017. Although some of its buildings have seen vandalism, Upper Heyford's runways are now a haven for wildlife, including peregrine falcons and buzzards. (Richard E. Flagg)

2. Upper Heyford

Another airfield that has also experienced its fair share of neglect is Upper Heyford. Refurbished after the war to receive SAC aircraft, it then played host to the first F-4 Phantoms to arrive in the UK, as well as B-52s, SR-71s and F-111s. Now known as Heyford Park, a number of its buildings remain in use for light industry, storage and technology. There is also a small museum located in what used to be the base commander's building. Again, however, many of Upper Heyford's long-since vacated buildings have become targets for those who fail to appreciate its historical significance.

3. Greenham Common

One airfield that courted much negative post-war publicity was Greenham Common. Despite its controversial use in later years, the airfield had been the setting for a momentous event when the first American paratroopers took off for Normandy at the start of the Allied invasion in June 1944. It was at Greenham Common that General Dwight D. Eisenhower addressed his troops in the evening before D-Day. Originally built in 1942, the airfield was returned to the Americans in 1950 and used as a primary base for SAC's bombers and tankers. By the 1980s, it was equipped with the first Tomahawk cruise missiles, thus sparking the protests that persisted for almost twenty years. Following the end of the Cold War, Greenham Common was handed back to the UK MoD in February 1992 and declared surplus to requirement. Today, the base has been turned into an extensive industrial estate, although it is also frequently used as a film location, appearing in promotional music videos and the 2015 film *Star Wars: The Force Awakens*.

Graffiti at RAF Greenham Common has its origins in the units that were stationed at the base. Here, Building 303, a maintenance hangar on the airfield's technical site, still retained some original artwork until it was demolished in 2013. (Richard E. Flagg)

4 and 5. Woodbridge and Bentwaters

With the departure of the USAF from Woodbridge, the base was divided into two sections and renamed Woodbridge Airfield and Rock Barracks – both areas being turned over to elements of the British Army. Its near neighbour, RAF Bentwaters, which had been vacated

Despite being closed to air traffic in 1993, Woodbridge still retains 95 per cent of its runway and taxiways. In 2016, the airfield was briefly used to test the new Airbus A400M Atlas. (Richard E. Flagg)

3 miles north-east of Woodbridge, Bentwaters also retains much of its infrastructure. With numerous buildings still remaining, the site is often used for the recording of television programmes and Hollywood films. (Richard E. Flagg)

by the USAF in 1993, saw a fitting tribute unveiled in 2007 when the Bentwaters Cold War Museum opened its doors to the public. Commemorating Bentwaters' 'twin base' story with RAF Woodbridge, the museum continues to pay homage to the air-sea rescue operations of the latter, as well as the former's very own 81st TFW.

6. Bruntingthorpe

Bruntingthorpe is also one of the more fortunate survivors of its past. Having been opened as an RAF training base during November 1942, it became part of the four-base USAF complex comprising Alconbury, Chelveston and Molesworth. In 1962, after nine years under USAF control, the facility was passed to the British MoD. Areas of the base were then sold off, while many buildings – including those used to test Frank Whittle's Meteor turbojet engine – were demolished. Nevertheless, Bruntingthorpe's 2-mile runway and many of its dispersal pads remain, along with two hangars used by SAC during the 1950s. Today, the Bruntingthorpe Aircraft Museum contains a variety of taxiable English Electric Lightnings, maintained by the Lightning Preservation Group.

7. Shepherds Grove

Originally known as Hepworth, Shepherds Grove had been built for the USAAF in 1943, although work was suspended that year to speed up construction at other airfields. Shepherds Grove was never used by the Eighth Air Force, but it was eventually loaned to the USAF in 1951. It subsequently housed F-86 Sabres (the first to arrive in the UK) until they were moved to Bentwaters. By 1958, all flying had ceased at the base and it was turned over to the RAF as a Thor missile site. After their removal in 1963, the airfield then reverted to agriculture. Today, just 5 per cent of its runways and taxiways remain, although some of its technical buildings are still used for light industry.

An aerial view of Bruntingthorpe taken in 2017. With its 10,000-foot runway still remaining, Bruntingthorpe Aerodrome was home to the only airworthy Vulcan, XH558, until it left for Doncaster Sheffield Airport. Bruntingthorpe is now home to the Lightning Preservation Group. (Airfield Research Group)

An image of Shepherds Grove's gymnasium and chancel building taken in 2008. Just under three-quarters of its buildings remain in use for storage and light industry. (Richard E. Flagg)

The Allied Air Forces Memorial Garden adjacent to Manston's airfield. Although the airport is now closed, it is a site marked with numerous memorials to those who served and many who fell. (Richard E. Flagg)

8. Manston

Following its illustrious Battle of Britain history, Manston became an 'emergency landing ground' in 1943, together with Woodbridge and Carnaby. After use with SAC and the USAF, the airfield was passed to RAF Fighter Command in June 1958. It then became a joint civilian and RAF airport during the 1960s, before eventually becoming Kent International Airport in 1989. Sadly, however, the airport closed twenty-five years later. Today, two museums remember Kent's most famous and historic airfield: the RAF Manston History Museum, and the Spitfire and Hurricane Memorial Museum.

9. Wyton

Wyton had an intermittent relationship with the USAF. It was from here that the first RAF aircraft to cross the German frontier (a Bristol Blenheim) took off on the day that Britain declared war. A major rotational base for SAC from November 1951, Wyton was then used sporadically, including for a four-month period in August 1989 when A-10 Thunderbolts from nearby Alconbury used it while resurfacing work was carried out at their home base. Today, Wyton's airfield has been decommissioned, but the support buildings are still used by elements of the British Army, including the Defence Infrastructure Organisation, which manages accommodation for American forces in the UK.

Wyton's decommissioned Watch Office and Met Section taken in 2015. Wyton was chiefly used by the RAF throughout its long history, but hosted elements of the USAF from the 1950s. (Richard E. Flagg)

An aerial shot of RAF Bassingbourn taken in 2009. Home to the famous B-17 *Memphis Belle*, Bassingbourn remained a training base for the British Army until its closure in 2014. (Richard E. Flagg)

10. Bassingbourn

Unlike most Second World War USAAF airfields, Bassingbourn in Cambridgeshire enjoyed an extended association with the Americans. Originally allocated to the Eighth Air Force during the Second World War, it was home to the famous B-17 *Memphis Belle* – the highly publicised heavy bomber flown by the first Eighth Air Force combat crewmen to reach their stipulated twenty-five missions. Bassingbourn also served as the headquarters of the 1st Combat Bombardment Wing of the 1st Division, before being upgraded after the war to receive SAC's B-29 and B-50 Superfortresses. Deployments were brief and Bassingbourn was handed back to the RAF, which used it for operational conversion to the English Electric Canberra. In 2014 the site was closed as a British Army training location and today it houses the Tower Museum, which is dedicated to all aspects of the airfield's history.

11. Brize Norton

As one of the four 'midland' group of bases, RAF Brize Norton's association with SAC began in the 1950s. By April 1965, SAC's temporary duty rotations had finished and the base was returned to the RAF. Today, Brize Norton is the RAF's largest air station and sole embarkation point for British troops deploying from the UK by air.

An RAF Airbus A400M Atlas undergoes maintenance in one of Brize Norton's hangars in 2015. From 1952 until 1965, the RAF's largest station played host to numerous USAF aircraft, including the B-47 and B-52. (Richard E. Flagg)

RAF Scampton remains an operational station and is home to world-famous RAF Aerobatic Team the Red Arrows. An Emergency War Plan Airfield, Scampton hosted the 28th Bomb Group's B-29 Superfortresses for a brief period between 1948 and 1949. (Author's Collection)

The last USAAF station to be passed back to the RAF in 1946, RAF Honington closed to flying just under fifty years later. Today, it is home to the RAF Regiment, which uses many of its existing hangars for storage and parades.

12. Scampton

Another iconic RAF airfield – Scampton – became part of a network of Emergency War Plan Airfields after the end of the Second World War. For a brief period between 1948 and 1949, this 'expansion scheme' airfield, which had launched the famous 'Dambusters' raid in 1943, was used by SAC's B-29 Superfortresses. Today, Scampton's historic standing is upheld by the RAF Aerobatic Team the Red Arrows, whose BAE Systems Hawks are the only permanent aircraft based on the station. However, in July 2018, the British Government announced that Scampton would be disposed of by 2022.

13. Honington

Another 'expansion scheme' airfield largely associated with the RAF since the Second World War is Honington. Now home to the RAF Regiment, the airfield was allocated to the Eighth Air Force in June 1942 as a major repair facility for its heavy bombers. It subsequently became the last USAAF station to be returned to the RAF in 1946. Today, many wartime buildings still survive within its perimeter.

14. North Pickenham

North Pickenham, the last airfield to be handed over to the USAAF during the Second World War, was returned to the RAF in August 1945. In 1954, its administration was briefly transferred back to the USAF, although it was never used. However, Thor missiles were supplied by the Americans in 1958 to complement the RAF's V-bombers during their development. Much like Greenham Common, however, a major CND protest led to the missile site's dismantling in 1963. Subsequently used to test Hawker Siddeley's P.1127

RAF North Pickenham was the last airfield to be handed to the USAAF during the Second World War. Today, half of its runways remain, providing space for the world's largest turkey farm, operated by Bernard Matthews plc. (Richard E. Flagg)

Kestrel (forerunner to the Harrier Jump Jet), North Pickenham eventually closed to flying in 1967. Today, it holds a Guinness World Record for being the site of the world's largest turkey farm, with approximately one million turkeys residing along its three surviving runways.

15. Hardwick

Hardwick's claim to fame lay in the 396 missions carried out by the 93rd Bomb Group between December 1942 and June 1945 – the most of any group of the Eighth Air Force. Today, Hardwick retains just under half of its runway layout and even less of its dispersed domestic sites. Nevertheless, the 93rd Bombardment Group museum maintains its displays in three Nissen huts located near Hardwick's Airfield Farm.

16. Lashenden

Due to the very nature of their existence, almost nothing remains of the prototype Advanced Landing Grounds (ALGs) established in Kent during 1944. Only Lashenden (confusingly called Headcorn Aerodrome today, although it has no connection to the wartime Headcorn ALG) betrays its wartime existence. Around 50 per cent of its grass runways are still in use for light aviation. The site's Lashenden Air Warfare Museum contains a small collection of aircraft wrecks and exhibits, including a piloted V1 Flying Bomb.

Although Hardwick still retains some of its runway layout and several Nissen huts (now home to the 93rd Bombardment Group Museum), many buildings have vanished. This image shows one of the last remaining temporary brick buildings. (Andy Laing)

Lashenden's main runway, pictured in 2013. By its very nature as an Advanced Landing Ground (ALG), Lashenden was only meant to be temporary. However, in the late 1960s, aviation returned to an airfield now confusingly called Headcorn (another Kent ALG). (Richard E. Flagg)

RAF Christchurch never survived the passage of time. Another Advanced Landing Ground (ALG), it became an aircraft production facility after the war. Once home to British aircraft designers, the airfield is now an industrial estate with no discernible features. (Author's Collection)

17. Christchurch

Another ALG sited along the coast in Dorset, Christchurch managed to survive longer than most. Handed to the Ministry of Aircraft Production after the war, Christchurch was then used by Airspeed Limited to develop its prototype airliner, the Ambassador. The airfield then hosted de Havilland, which developed the military jet fighters Vampire and Sea Vixen. A concrete runway using the former wartime square mesh track was laid for the purpose. Sadly, a reduction in military contracts then led to the airfield's closure, which was finally demolished in 1966. Today, a housing estate (with roads named in honour of British aviation) and the Runway Industrial Park are the only reminders of the airfield's existence.

An airfield structure that has stood the test of time. Debach's runways may have disintegrated soon after its opening, but its control tower remains on solid ground thanks to the hard work of the 493rd Bomb Group 'Helton's Hellcats' Museum. (Richard E. Flagg)

18. Debach

One airfield whose name baffled its American tenants was Debach (pronounced 'Deb-idge' by local inhabitants). 'Dee-bark' (as the Americans called it) was the last Eighth Air Force heavy bomber base to become fully operational. Initially, its runways deteriorated to such an extent that it was forced to temporarily close just eight months after it had been opened. Following the war, Debach was first used as a German prisoner of war camp, then a site for those displaced by wartime bombing. Today, just 5 per cent of its runways and taxiways remain in place, although its control tower is still standing thanks to a painstaking restoration undertaken by volunteers of the 493rd Bomb Group 'Helton's Hellcats' Museum.

19. Harrington

Harrington in Northamptonshire was abandoned in the 1960s, but has since been protected under Listed Building status after serving as a Thor missile site during the Cold War. Much of its runways and hardstands were broken up shortly after it was decommissioned, but its missile launch pads remain distinctly visible. Its most famous residents, the 'Carpetbaggers', are commemorated by the Harrington Aviation Museum, which was formed in 1993 to commemorate the USAAF's unique 801st and 492nd Bomb Groups.

Although its Thor missile site received Grade II listed status in 2011, Harrington's runways and dispersals have all but disappeared. A far cry from its time as the base of the 'Carpetbaggers'. (Barrington Williams)

An aerial view of Sculthorpe taken in 2009. Remarkably intact, the airfield is still in use with the USAF today – although only for low-flying training exercises and airdrops. (Richard E. Flagg)

20. Sculthorpe

Sculthorpe enjoyed a long association with the USAF throughout the Cold War and beyond. Originally built in 1942, the airfield was occupied by the USAF from January 1949. During the 1980s, it was categorised as a 'stand-by' station, with its runways being used by various USAF units while their home base runways were being resurfaced. In recent years, Sculthorpe has been used as an army helicopter training zone and an area for military exercises. Today, the airfield remains largely intact, although its five hangars were demolished in 2009.

21. Marham

Like Sculthorpe, Marham was made available to the USAF shortly after the Second World War. As the headquarters of the Third Air Division in 1948, Marham was at the forefront of B-29 Superfortress operations in the UK. However, it was returned to RAF control two years later. Today, Marham is home to the RAF's Tornado Force, which will soon be making way for the arrival of the next generation of jet fighter. In preparation for its conversion to the new F-35 Lightning, the airfield is currently undergoing extensive reconstruction. Marham's main runway has been rebuilt and fittingly received the first four F-35s on 6 June 2018 – the 74th anniversary of D-Day.

The past, present and future of RAF Marham in one image. One of the first B-29 Superfortress bases in the late 1940s, Marham continues to be the leading edge of British military aviation. (Richard E. Flagg)

The American-built RAF Stansted Mountfitchet has been swallowed by Britain's fourth busiest airport, London Stansted. Around twenty-four million people per year now take off from a main runway first built seventy-five years ago. (Author's Collection)

22. Stansted Mountfitchet

A complete facelift took place at Stansted Mountfitchet during the late 1980s, when the airfield – then called Stansted Airport – was redeveloped to become London's third international airport. Having been the largest Ninth Air Force base in East Anglia, it was then used as an RAF storage depot and German prisoner of war camp, before being taken over by the Ministry of Civil Aviation in 1949. Six years later, American engineers arrived to extend the runway for possible use by NATO, which never materialised. Instead, Stansted was subsequently used by holiday charter operators, before receiving a £100 million upgrade in 1988. Stansted has since become the UK's fourth busiest airport.

23. Ridgewell

Lying beneath the approach path to Stansted are the remnants of Essex's only long-term heavy bomber airfield, Ridgewell. Following the USAAF's departure in June 1945, the airfield was handed over to the RAF's Nos 94 and 95 Maintenance Units for the storage and disposal of unused ordnance. For thirteen years, its three runways were lined with thousands of Allied bombs. In 1957, the facility was decommissioned and its runways and hardstands were broken up. Both wartime hangars were dismantled during the 1980s after extensive use as storage facilities by USAF units based at nearby Wethersfield. Today, just 5 per cent of Ridgewell's airfield remains, although public roads around the site are said to use more old taxiways than any other Eighth Air Force base. The Ridgewell Airfield

The western edge of RAF Ridgewell's perimeter track – now a public road. Essex's only long-term heavy bomber base provides more public highways than any other former Eighth Air Force base. (Richard E. Flagg)

Commemorative Association pays tribute to Ridgewell's 381st Bomb Group with a display of memorabilia housed in a surviving Nissen hut on the airfield's former hospital site.

24. Wethersfield

Just 5 miles south-west of Ridgewell is the former RAF Wethersfield. After an extensive association with the USAAF and USAF, it was returned to the RAF in July 1990. However, its housing remained in use for USAF personnel stationed at Alconbury, Molesworth and Upwood. The following year, the entire site was turned over to the Ministry of Defence Police, which commenced training activities in April 1993. Wethersfield now serves as the combined headquarters and training centre for the Ministry of Defence Police, although it was announced in 2016 that the site would be sold in order to reduce the MoD estate. Nevertheless, Wethersfield's infrastructure remains largely intact; its complete post-war runway and both hangars still exist, while the Wethersfield Airfield Museum is housed in one of its many surviving buildings.

25. Andrews Field

6 miles further south lies Andrews Field – the first airfield built by American engineering battalions during the Second World War. When the airfield was returned to the British in 1945, it was used by the RAF's first fighter jet, the Gloster Meteor. By 1949, however, much of the airfield had been abandoned, with some of its buildings being used for temporary housing. Although its American-built runways were removed after the war, aviation returned to the site in 1972 when a grass strip was laid along the line of its main runway. Today, this former wartime airfield is home to the Andrewsfield Flying Club, which commemorates its USAAF connection through artwork and photographs displayed on its clubhouse walls.

Lying on the approach path to Stansted Airport, RAF Wethersfield has all the attributes to be a live airfield. Now used by the Ministry of Defence Police, the airfield still hosts aviation in the form of No. 614 Volunteer Gliding Squadron RAF. (Richard E. Flagg)

Pictured in 2010, the first airfield constructed by American engineers during the Second World War still retains part of its outline. Andrews Field is now home to the Andrewsfield Flying Club. (Richard E. Flagg)

26. Cheddington

Following the Second World War, Cheddington in Buckinghamshire continued living a 'cloak and dagger' existence. Transferred to the USAAF in September 1942, it was largely used to deliver propaganda leaflets, as well as members of the Special Operations Executive to parts of Nazi-occupied Europe. Post-war, the British Army used the site until its closure in 1952. However, it has since been alleged that the site continued to be used by the US Central Intelligence Agency for 'behind the lines' resistance activities during the Cold War. Today, many of its buildings still remain, including a number of ammunition blocks, which reputedly held a store of Soviet Bloc small arms.

Cheddington bears little resemblance from its time as a wartime airfield. Small areas still remain, including this – the remnants of a Nissen hut photographed in 2010. Nevertheless, some important buildings still survive. (Ricky Day)

27. Bovingdon

Located just 10 miles south-east of Cheddington are the extensive remains of RAF Bovingdon. Opened in June 1942, Bovingdon was used as both a Combat Crew Replacement Centre and base for the European Air Transport Service, which returned thousands of Americans to the USA during the Second World War. Bovingdon also served as the base for General Eisenhower's personal B-17, and as the training facility for a group of journalists (including Walter Cronkite), who flew an Eighth Air Force mission to Germany on 26 February 1943. Following the war, the USAF returned to Bovingdon, where Douglas C-47 Skytrains were assigned to support the nearby Third Air Force headquarters at RAF South Ruislip. In later years, Bovingdon was used in the production of several war films, including the 1968 technicolour movie *Battle of Britain*. Today, the former airfield is used as both a prison and venue for a weekly public market. A VHF Omni-Directional Range beacon on the ground at Bovingdon also maintains a 'stacking' area overhead for aircraft approaching London's Heathrow Airport.

28. 'Pinetree'

11 miles to the south-west, Wycombe Abbey (a school that was founded in 1896) barely hints at its wartime past. Once 'the largest switchboard in England', Wycombe Abbey was 'Pinetree' – the headquarters of VIII Bomber Command, and the eventual 'nerve centre' of the Eighth Air Force. Today, despite having its extensive underground bunker sealed off, this stately home still retains rooms where planning for early Eighth Air Force raids took place.

Bovingdon still retains half of its runway infrastructure, although many of its wartime buildings have since been demolished. Its wartime control tower still stands, despite being neglected. (Julian Mcmorine)

Wycombe Abbey still retains its splendour, although its time as 'England's largest switchboard' is long-since gone. Today, it is a 'world leader in girls' boarding education'. (J. Ross Greene)

29. Kimbolton

As one of the USAAF's first heavy bomber bases, Kimbolton in Cambridgeshire initially hosted the 91st Bomb Group in 1942. However, its insufficient runway length meant that it was quickly passed to the 17th Bomb Group, which briefly used the airfield for its medium bomber operations prior to departing for North Africa. After extensions were made to the main runway, the 379th Bomb Group arrived at Kimbolton in May 1943. Its B-17s ultimately

Imprints of a workman's boots set in stone at RAF Kimbolton. One of the USAAF's first heavy bomber bases, Kimbolton has lost 95 per cent of its infrastructure to time and the elements. (Airfield Research Group)

dropped a greater bomb tonnage than any other group before moving on to North Africa, where it was deactivated. After the war, Kimbolton was passed to the RAF, which used it for basic training. Since its deactivation in the 1950s, however, the airfield layout has been used by the Hunts Kart Racing Club, whose club flag commemorates the airfield's heritage with a triangle surrounding the letter 'K' – the wartime identifier for the 379th's B-17s.

30. Little Staughton

Another early Eighth Air Force heavy bomber base, Little Staughton, still retains much of its infrastructure. One of the airfields surveyed by the USAAC in October 1941, Little Staughton was eventually used for heavy maintenance. Following the end of the Second World War, the USAF returned to extend its main runway for use in the event of emergency. However, the potential never became a reality. Today, its control tower remains, as well as three of its eleven hangars, plus a sizeable portion of its main runway.

31. Thurleigh

Less than 5 miles away, Thurleigh boasts even more substantial remains. Like Little Staughton, Thurleigh was inspected by USAAC personnel in 1941 and found to be inadequate for use by American heavy bombers. Its runways were duly lengthened and strengthened in preparation for the arrival of the 306th Bomb Group's B-17s, which remained at Thurleigh until December 1945. As a result, the 306th enjoyed the longest tenure of any USAAF group at a UK base. Following the war, Thurleigh underwent extensive reconstruction to become the Royal Aircraft Establishment, Bedford. Despite

A German-built Aquila A 210 aircraft taxis past Little Staughton's Grade II listed control tower. Light aviation still takes place at Little Staughton thanks to the Light Aircraft Association. (Richard E. Flagg)

An aerial view of RAF Thurleigh taken in 2009. Occupied by the 306th Bomb Group (the longest tenure of any USAAF group at a UK base), Thurleigh became the Royal Aircraft Establishment, Bedford. Twenty-one years after its closure, Thurleigh retains just over half of its original infrastructure. (Richard E. Flagg)

closure in 1997, Thurleigh still retains much of its original features, including the entire length of its main runway, which is now used for the storage of new cars. The 306th Bombardment Group Museum, located in the wartime Arms and Ammunition Store, commemorates the history of Thurleigh's so-called 'Reich Wreckers'.

32. Chelveston

A few miles further on, Chelveston is now home to the Chelveston Renewable Energy Park, with its array of solar panels and wind turbines. Originally a collection of short grass runways, the airfield was upgraded to 'Class A' standard and turned over to the USAAF in 1942. After hosting a number of troop carrier and bomb groups, the airfield was returned to the RAF in October 1945. However, after seven years, Chelveston welcomed back an American engineering

Solar panels and wind turbines adorn RAF Chelveston today. Once the home of the longest runway in the UK (its straight line still visible), Chelveston has since made way for renewable energy. (Airfield Research Group)

battalion, which extended the runway to make it the longest in the UK. Ten years later, the airfield's use came to a close when the USAF's B-66s departed for Europe. Nevertheless, when American forces were forced to return from France, it became a USAF storage facility. By 1977, amid budget cuts, the MoD closed the facility and its infrastructure was broken up to bolster other civil engineering projects in Northamptonshire. Today, the airfield has virtually vanished, although the imprint of its runway still remains visible from the air. A memorial to the various units stationed at RAF Chelveston was unveiled in 2007.

33. Podington

Another Northamptonshire airfield located just 6 miles south-west of Chelveston (as the bomber flies), Podington has retained much of its original features. Built between 1940 and 1941, it was made available to the USAAF in April 1942. Podington was originally home to the 15th Bombardment Squadron – the first bomb unit to arrive in the UK. However, the 15th's stay was short and Podington briefly hosted a Combat Crew Replacement Unit. Subsequently upgraded to 'Class A' standard, the airfield was then temporarily used by the 100th Bomb Group, before being handed to the 92nd – the oldest of the Eighth Air Force's first heavy bomb groups (and first to make the Transatlantic crossing). As a result, the 92nd became known as 'Fame's Favored Few'. After the war, Podington was returned to the UK MoD, which used it to store millions of wartime

Few former USAAF airfields have been used like Podington. Santa Pod – Europe's first permanent drag racing venue – opened in 1966. Today, it hosts the British and European Drag Racing Championships. (Author's Collection)

A stained glass window at St James the Apostle Church commemorates the 384th Bomb Group, which was based at nearby RAF Grafton Underwood from June 1943. (Andy Laing)

sandbags. After being sold to private investors in the early 1960s, the airfield's runway was then quickly purloined by a group of drag-racing enthusiasts. Today, the Santa Pod Raceway continues to host the FIA European Drag Racing Championships, as well as over fifty car events each year.

34. Grafton Underwood

Grafton Underwood, 13 miles to the north, has led a much quieter existence since its time as the first British airfield to launch an American heavy bomber mission. Originally home to the 15th Bombardment Squadron (before its move to Molesworth and Podington), Grafton Underwood then hosted two squadrons of the 97th Bomb Group, which flew the first heavy bomber raid on 17 August 1942. After accommodating a number of other groups, the airfield was returned to the RAF after the war and used for the storage and maintenance of thousands of Air Ministry vehicles. It was then declared surplus to requirement in February 1959 and returned to agriculture. Large sections of its concreted areas were subsequently removed, although its wooded areas are now open to the public as picnic sites. During the 1990s, a memorial was unveiled to the 384th Bomb Group, which used the airfield for the majority of its existence. One side of the monument simply reads: 'The first and last bombs dropped by the 8th Air Force were from airplanes flying from Grafton Underwood.'

35. Prestwick

As well as being the only place in the UK where Elvis Presley was known to have set foot, RAF Prestwick in Scotland was also the location for the arrival of the first 'big tail' B-17 on British soil during 'Operation BOLERO'. A year later, the first glider (towed by a Dakota of RAF Transport Command) touched down after a long flight from Canada. Used as a major Transatlantic Ferry Terminal throughout the war and into the mid-1960s, RAF Prestwick eventually became Glasgow Prestwick Airport, and in terms of passenger traffic is now Scotland's fifth busiest airport.

An aerial view of Glasgow Prestwick Airport, currently Scotland's fifth busiest airport. Used throughout 'Operation BOLERO' and beyond, Prestwick was eventually vacated by the USAF in 1966. (Michael Stalker)

36. Valley

RAF Valley in Wales was opened as an RAF Fighter Sector Station in February 1941. Two years later, with its runways and taxiways extended, it became a USAAF Ferry Terminal, handling American arrivals from their Transatlantic flights. It is said that on one day alone in September 1944, the airfield handled ninety-nine B-17s and B-24s that had been ferried in from Iceland. Today, RAF Valley continues to host military aviation. Home to the RAF's No. 4 Flying Training School, it is also the base for the Mountain Rescue Service.

37. Nutts Corner

115 miles across the Irish Sea, RAF Nutts Corner near Belfast had been used by Coastal Command for maritime patrols in the North Atlantic. By August 1942, it was allocated to the Eighth Air Force as a bomber training base, before being used as a major transportation hub for USAAF B-17s flying the Transatlantic Supply Route. Post-war, with the start of civil air operations, Nutts Corner became known as Belfast-Nutts Corner Airport. However, due to mountains and obstacles in its vicinity, the steep approach path necessary to reach the airport rendered it unsuitable and it was closed in the early 1960s. Today, its runways still exist and are used for stock car racing and are the site for a weekly market.

Today, RAF Valley remains an active RAF station and still retains its original runway layout. During the Second World War, it was a prime transit hub for American bombers arriving in Great Britain. (Author's Collection)

After becoming a civil airport, RAF Nutts Corner was closed in the 1960s. Its runway layout, extant since 1940, now plays host to a Sunday market and a stock car racing circuit. (Author's Collection)

Regarded as the largest military airfield in Europe during the Second World War, Burtonwood has seen its layout sliced by the M62 motorway. This 2001 image shows the last remaining part of the main runway before it was broken up. (Author's Collection)

38. Burtonwood

Around 170 miles away, RAF Burtonwood in Lancashire has effectively been sliced in two by the M62 motorway. The largest military airfield in Europe during the Second World War (and Military Air Transport Service terminal until 1958), Burtonwood was eventually returned to the British MoD in 1965. Nevertheless, with the transfer of stores and equipment from France during 1966, the airfield was turned over to the US Army as a storage and logistics depot. With the end of the Cold War, Burtonwood was declared surplus to NATO requirements and closed in 1994. Today, part of the airfield is occupied by a motorway service area, while most of its associated infrastructure has been demolished. However, Burtonwood's remarkable existence is commemorated by the RAF Burtonwood Heritage Centre, located just off the M62 on its former domestic Site Four.

39. Polebrook

Many firsts are associated with RAF Polebrook. One of the first installations inspected by the Americans in 1941, it also became the first airfield to welcome the first B-17 Flying Fortress, before launching the first American heavy bomber raid (together with Grafton Underwood) in August 1942. Polebrook was also linked with the movie industry. When RAF No. 90 Squadron was resident in 1941, the movie *Flying Fortress* was filmed at Polebrook. The airfield then went on to host movie star Clark Gable, who arrived in 1943 to produce a training and recruitment film. Like many Eighth Air Force bases, Polebrook was handed to RAF Maintenance Command in July 1945 and for four years became the base for a Thor missile squadron. Today, the airfield is almost unrecognisable, although one of its hangars still exists. A memorial to Polebrook's final USAAF residents – the 351st Bomb Group – acknowledges the sacrifices of its crews and the 175 aircraft that never returned.

Pictured in 2009, this image shows the remnants of Polebrook's runway threshold. Except for one hangar, almost nothing remains of an airfield that played a starring role in the early days of the USAAF's presence in the UK. (Richard E. Flagg)

Over three-quarters of a century on from the first USAAF arrival in the UK, the modern-day USAF maintains its legacy on British soil. Ten long-standing UK airfields and several non-flying facilities now host some 24,000 personnel, civilian staff and family members.

40. RAF Menwith Hill

RAF Menwith Hill, near Harrogate in North Yorkshire, is a non-flying, multi-service communications and intelligence base. Opened in 1954, it is manned by some 2,500 staff, including those of the USAF. Today, its golf ball-like radomes are believed to be capable of downloading up to two million conversations per hour.

41. RAF Fylingdales

Just under 50 miles to the north-east are the ball-shaped listening posts of RAF Fylingdales. Located deep in the North Yorkshire moors, Fylingdales provides a continuous ballistic missile early warning service monitored by some 350 staff, including a USAF liaison officer.

42 and 43. RAF Croughton and RAF Barford St John

RAFs Croughton and Barford St John have been non-flying USAF bases for more than sixty years. The latter, in Oxfordshire, was used to test Britain's first generation of jet fighters, while the former (initially named RAF Brackley) served mainly as a Northamptonshire training base for the Glider Pilot Regiment during the Second World War. Today, Croughton and Barford St John are used by the USAF as signal relay stations, with Croughton providing command, control and communications to a number of military and civilian agencies across Europe. It also provides combat support to neighbouring Fairford and Welford.

44. RAF Welford

The Berkshire airfield of RAF Welford opened in 1943 and was used by the USAAF's Ninth Air Force as a troop carrier airfield during the Second World War. Once the owner of its very own M4 access road, Welford is no longer an active airfield, but the largest USAF weapons store in Western Europe, and a major maintenance hub.

45. RAF Fairford

Just over 20 miles from Welford, RAF Fairford remains a standby airfield for USAF and NATO forces. Although it has no permanently assigned aircraft, the base is retained as a 'combat ready' location, able to receive and support any operational units or training exercises. When NASA's Space Shuttle was in operation, Fairford was the UK's only

Currently a standby airfield, RAF Fairford still sees regular visits by elements of the USAF, including B-52s. Here, a Rockwell B-1 Lancer is being prepared for an exercise in the summer of 2017. (Richard E. Flagg)

An aerial view of Alconbury's runway taken in 2016. Although the airfield is being developed for business and housing, the main support areas are still staffed by USAF personnel. (Richard E. Flagg)

Transatlantic Abort Landing site. It also remains the USAF's only European airfield for heavy bombers thanks to its runway's unrestricted load-bearing capacity – a runway that has also assisted units from other airfields, including Mildenhall and Brize Norton, on the occasions their runways have required resurfacing. Fairford is also home to the Royal International Air Tattoo – the world's largest military air show.

46. RAF Alconbury

Although RAF Alconbury's airfield and its associated infrastructure were returned to the UK MoD in 1995, its main base support areas have remained under USAF control. Administrative and financial offices are still manned by USAF personnel, while its housing and base exchange continue to sustain those personnel stationed on the base and at Molesworth.

One of the Eighth Air Force's first bases, Molesworth was eventually used to store Ground Launched Cruise Missiles (GLCM) in the 1980s. Pictured in 2016, Molesworth's GCLM storage igloos are still overlooked by a surveillance tower. (Richard E. Flagg)

Today, RAF Feltwell is administered by a space control intelligence arm of the USAF. It is also used as a housing estate for personnel based at both RAF Mildenhall and RAF Lakenheath. (Richard E. Flagg)

47. RAF Molesworth

Molesworth, one of the Eighth Air Force's earliest stations, and home to the 15th Bomb Squadron, which carried out the USAAF's first European bombing raid of the Second World War, still houses elements of the USAF. These units continue to provide intelligence support for US and NATO missions in Europe and the Middle East, while providing global assistance in the 'War on Terror'. Despite their ongoing work, both Alconbury and Molesworth face closure over the next decade.

48. RAF Feltwell

RAF Feltwell in Norfolk is a direct associate of both Lakenheath and Mildenhall, accommodating many of its service personnel. An 'expansion period' airfield constructed in the late 1930s, Feltwell hosted heavy bombers during the Second World War, before becoming a Thor missile site during the Cuban Missile Crisis. It went on to become a facility that tracked and adjusted the trajectory of satellites between 1989 and 2003. In addition to its current role as a housing estate for USAF personnel, it also provides leadership training for US airmen and women.

49. RAF Lakenheath

Today, RAF Lakenheath is the jewel in the USAF's British crown. It serves as the largest USAF base in the UK and is home to USAFE-AFAFRICA's sole F-15 fighter wing – the 48th Fighter Wing (more commonly known as the 'Liberty Wing' thanks to its wartime feats over France). Lakenheath is home to some 4,500 active-duty military personnel, as well as 1,000 British and American civilians. Since 1960, it has provided worldwide responsive combat airpower and support.

50. RAF Mildenhall

Although facing closure in the coming years, Lakenheath's nearest neighbour, RAF Mildenhall, remains one of the longest-serving active military stations in the UK. Its resident 100th Air Refuelling Wing (100th ARW) owes its legacy to the Eighth Air Force's 100th Bomb Group (100th BG) – more commonly known as 'The Bloody Hundredth', after it was decimated by the Luftwaffe during the Second World War. Today, the 100th ARW's KC-135 Stratotankers' tails

An F-15 Strike Eagle of the 48th FW touches down at Lakenheath after a training sortie. Lakenheath has been home to the 'Liberty Wing' since 1960 and is the USAF's largest UK base today. (Richard E. Flagg)

are decorated with the 100th BG's identifier – the letter 'D' surrounded by a square. It is the only modern-day USAF operational wing allowed to display the code of its wartime predecessor.

Three-quarters of a century after the Second World War ended, and despite the continued presence of American military aviation on British soil today, a remarkable history is dissolving into the landscape. While some former airfields have remained visible in the years since the end of the Second World War, others have been erased by time or the plough. It is a transformation best encapsulated in the words of one USAAF veteran who returned to his base many years later. They are words that could speak for many US Air Force bases in the UK:

> The site had long since returned to grain fields. Two old hangars were still standing, but they were now filled with farm machinery. They had traded airplanes for tractors! Part of me knew this was as it should be ... to me, it represented the most intensely lived year of my life. To me this was ground as hallowed as Lincoln's Gettysburg ... it was from here that I had the first traumatic shock of combat. It was from here that so many of my friends, some of the finest men I have ever known, began their last flight.

A Boeing KC-135 Stratotanker of the 351st Air Refuelling Squadron, 100th Air Refuelling Wing (100th ARW), pictured at Mildenhall in 2016. The 100th ARW's aircraft bear the 'Square-D' identifier of its predecessor, the wartime 100th Bomb Group. (Richard E. Flagg)

A tractor sprays crops next to RAF Horham's main runway. Just one of scores of American wartime airfields throughout East Anglia, it was from here that the last B-17 to be shot down over Europe took off on 7 May 1945 – the day before VE Day.

Acknowledgements

My very special thanks go to Richard Flagg, without whom this book could not have been so extensively illustrated. His impressive collection of modern-day airfield photography can be found at www.ukairfields.org.uk.

To my wife, Aki, for her unwavering patience and understanding. As they say in Osaka – 'okini'.

Thanks also go to J. Ross Greene, for his advice, support and friendship. Brought together by the Eighth Air Force, ours is a contemporary example of the 'special relationship'. Thanks also to Paul Francis for his expert guidance and opinion. Archivist and director of the Airfield Research Group, Paul has written over 120 historical reports and eight books detailing military buildings, camps and airfields. To Paul Furlonger, for his valued support and encouragement.

Finally, to the men of the 381st Bombardment Group (Heavy), whose stories first set me on a journey of discovery. It is to them that this book is dedicated.

References

The following books and websites have proved invaluable during the course of my research and come highly recommended:

Baker, David, *USAF: 70 Years of the World's Most Powerful Air Force* (Mortons Media Group, 2017).

Clarke, Bob, *The Archaeology of Airfields* (The History Press, 2009).

Falconer, Jonathan, *RAF Airfields of World War 2* (Midland Publishing, 2012).

Francis, Paul; Flagg, Richard; Crisp, Graham, *Nine Thousand Miles of Concrete* (Historic England, 2016).

Freeman, Roger, *Airfields of the Eighth: Then and Now* (Battle of Britain International Ltd, 2006).

Freeman, Roger, *Airfields of the Ninth: Then and Now* (Battle of Britain Prints International Ltd, 1994).

Jackson, Robert, *United States Air Force in Britain* (Airlife Publishing Ltd, 2000).

www.ukairfields.org.uk

www.airfieldresearchgroup.org.uk

www.aviationtrails.wordpress.com